636.7
DUF   Duffy, Kyla

        Lost souls:Found!

                        $12.95

		DATE DUE		

Lost Souls: FOUND!™

Inspiring Stories About Dachshunds

Kyla Duffy and Lowrey Mumford

Published by Happy Tails Books™, LLC

Each "Lost Souls: Found!" book contains over 50 heart-warming short stories and anecdotes about dogs who were once in dire straits but have since been united with humans who love them. The stories lead you down a twisting and turning road of emotion, exposing the misery of neglect, the selflessness of rescue, and the joy these rehabilitated, "found" souls bring to their new families. You're sure to laugh and cry – and if you've had your own dog, you're in for some "mine does that too!" moments.

Lost Souls: FOUND!™

Inspiring Stories About Dachshunds by Kyla Duffy and Lowrey Mumford

Published by Happy Tails Books™, LLC   www.happytailsbooks.com

The publisher gratefully acknowledges the numerous Dachshund rescue groups and their members who generously granted permission to use their stories and photos.

Front cover photo:
　　Cinnamon, by Karen Taylor, www.pawsinthegarden.com
Back cover photos:
　　Jelly Bean, by Tiffany and Jared Ishiguro, www.style-ish.com (top)
　　Fred, by Courtney Po (right)
　　Thor, Napoleon Dynamite, and Fred by Courtney Po (center)
　　Rusty and Lila, by Nicole Smit (Left)
Interior photos unassociated with a story:
　　Interior Title Page: Macho, by Tiffany and Jared Ishiguro
　　P 7: By Ashley Johnson, www.ashleyjohnsonphotography.com
　　P 15: Linux and Rosie
　　P156: Sassy Sue, by Cara Christy

Publishers Cataloging In Publication

Lost Souls: FOUND!™ Inspiring Stories About Dachshunds/ [Compiled and edited by] Kyla Duffy and Lowrey Mumford.

p. ; cm.

ISBN: 978-0-9824895-2-9

1. Dachshund. 2. Dog rescue. 3. Dogs – Anecdotes. 4. Animal welfare – United States. 5. Human-animal relationships – Anecdotes. I. Duffy, Kyla. II. Mumford, Lowrey. III. Title.

SF426.5　2010
636.7538-dc21　2009909077

11- 772
HAPPY TAILS
(AmAZoN)
10/11
$12.95

Thank you to all of the contributors and rescue groups whose thought-provoking stories make this book come to life!

All American Dachshund Rescue
http://www.allamericandachshundrescue.org/

All Texas Dachshund Rescue
http://www.atdr.org/

Central Texas Dachshund Rescue
http://www.ctdr.org/

Coast to Coast Dachshund Rescue
http://www. c2cdr.org/

Dachshund Adoption, Rescue, & Education
http://www. daretorescue.com/

Dachshund Rescue of Houston
http://www.dachshundrescueofhouston.org/

Dachshund Rescue of North America
http://www.drna.org/

Diamond Dachshund Rescue of Texas
http://www. ddrtx.org/

Florida Dachshund Rescue, Inc.
http://www.fldr.org/

Midwest Dachshund Rescue
http://www. mwdr.org/

Oregon Dachshund Rescue
http://www. odr-inc.org/

Table of Contents

Introduction:
A Rescuer With Many Tails

One day, as I was getting ready for work with a half an eye on the news, a story suddenly caught my full attention: a group named DARE (Dachshund Adoption Rescue Education) had Dachshunds for *adoption*. Now, we've had a pack of Dachshunds since I was first married, and I guess I knew there were rescue groups out there, but I never gave it much thought.

A while later, after my senior, blind boy Buddy passed away, I was looking at classified ads for a puppy when I suddenly remembered DARE. Needless to say, that's where we found our next dog. I felt so good about adopting a dog-in-need and was instantly hooked on rescue, so when DARE asked if I would consider fostering, my answer was an enthusiastic *YES*!

Dachshunds come to DARE from breeders, shelters, and owners who surrender them due to unforeseen circumstances. Shelters sometimes have a hard time adopting out Doxies because many are considered aggressive, but we often find that in reality, they are just scared to death at the noisy shelter. With a little care, most Doxies quickly lose that aggressive behavior. I am very proud to say that DARE, like many other reputable rescues, doesn't discriminate on age, health, or social issues.

As rescuers, one of our toughest jobs is fostering senior Doxies who may just have a few days or weeks left to live.

It is heart-wrenching when any dog dies, but holding a dog in loving arms when he crosses over the Rainbow Bridge is always worth the emotional pain. Not all dogs that come into rescue are old or ill, and this sadness is balanced by the joys of placing healthy fosters into loving "forever homes."

I have to tell you a short story about Rusty, who came into DARE as a very young-looking, active 14-year-old. His owner had passed away, and the family did not want to keep him. At an adoption event, a senior couple, "The Goldies," were interested in my foster, Sadie, age seven, but they didn't have anyone to take her should they have to go into assisted living.

Instead, I suggested they might like to foster a Doxie: DARE would pay for medical expenses, and should something happen and they could no longer foster, DARE would place the dog elsewhere. They liked the idea and picked Rusty from the assortment of appropriate matches I offered. When I told them Rusty was used to sleeping in the "human bed" and sitting on the couch, Rusty's soon-to-be foster Mom's eyes grew as big as saucers and she said, "I don't know if I want him on the couch and in my bed..." Regardless, I wasn't worried.

That evening, Rusty walked right in to The Goldies' home and jumped up on the couch. He was home – it was obvious. But, to follow protocol, I explained that we would need to put his bio and picture on the website so he could be adopted. When I called later that week to check in and request information for the website, Mr. Goldie was suddenly very quiet. I asked what was wrong, and he said that he didn't think he could let Rusty go - they wanted to keep him.

It was like fireworks going off in my head – Mr. Goldie had said just what I needed to hear. Identifying the right family for the right dog is an art that foster parents learn, and I knew Rusty and The Goldies were a clear match from the start. Moments like that make it all worthwhile.

There are so many Dachshunds in need, and I am just one among many devoted volunteers who have given our hearts and souls to make a difference in their lives. Though difficult and draining at times, rescue is the most rewarding thing I can think to do with my life. I hope the stories in this book (from DARE and from many other rescues around the country) encourage *you* to consider making rescue a part of your life, too – whether in the form of volunteering your time and skills, donating to your favorite breed rescue, adopting your next dog, or just sharing information about adoption with friends and family. You, too, can experience the joy that those of us in rescue already know so well.

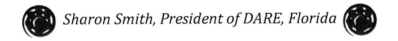

Sharon Smith, President of DARE, Florida

Inspiring Stories
About Dachshunds

Two for the Road

Dachshunds were bred to hunt badgers. Their name literally means "badger dog" in German. Because they were bred to go below ground, they have developed a couple of interesting characteristics.

Maybe you have noticed that Dachshunds have a bark that is disproportionate to their size. In other words, they're loud little men and women. The deep bark enabled hunters to know what was going on underground. Less obvious is their ability to "re-use" their own air. I discovered this after doing some research when my Dachshund went beneath lots of bedcovers in the winter and somehow didn't suffocate.

I look at my friend and can't imagine him in combat with a badger, even though he is a persistent fellow. The Hound of the Baskervilles might have had a chance, but not Smitty, my six-year-old, red, short-haired, purebred male. He is dashingly handsome and has endearing, cognac-colored eyes. He is in great health and form. Even so, battling a badger? I don't think so.

I don't know Smitty's entire history, but apparently it wasn't pleasant. I have a few theories that involve multiple owners. By the time I first saw him, his shelter crate had a number of warning stickers on it, identifying him as too difficult, or even dangerous, to handle and walk. He therefore spent an entire winter in his crate - becoming even more difficult.

My previous Dachshund, cleverly named Badger, lived a long and happy life. She was 15 when she died, and I had decided against another dog. But a good friend named Shannon, who is involved with Beagle rescue, practically insisted. She knows that I live a very solitary life that would be even more solitary without a K9 companion.

When Shannon and I went to the shelter together, Smitty was not thrilled to see me. Regardless, we took him for a walk, filled out the comprehensive questionnaire, three references were called, and out the door we went for a trial period. Eventually, Smitty (named after my father) and I became best friends.

Something *must* have happened to Smitty before I met him because he is indeed a problem child, but not with me. We are glued to each other. He has bedding in every room of my two-story house, a fenced yard, and I've even provided him with framed artwork at his eye level. He gets great veterinary care, two, three, even four walks a day, and many car rides.

I've spent a lot of money on behavioral modification specialists, DVDs, and books. But he is still mouth-aggressive with others; and he is not pleased to be around other dogs. Here's the punchline: We're two for the road. I've also spent a lot of money on DVDs, books, and therapists for *myself*.

Ultimately, I am a reclusive curmudgeon, a stick-in-the-mud, really, and while I don't exactly have mouth aggression, I have burned a lot of bridges in my lifetime. My behavior, however, is not a byproduct of an unfortunate childhood. No one abused me or neglected me. I was always loved and cared for, and I think that because I *was* loved and cared for, I can pass that on to Smitty - and, at the very least, he will have *my* full attention, a wonderful life, a healthy diet, and, in all likelihood, a lot of things that were missing in the first five years of his life.

"My little dog – a heartbeat at my feet." -Novelist Edith Wharton

 *Craig Marshall Smith*

He's Just Like Me

No one was more upset than our senior Dachshund Willie when our Beagle lost his battle with kidney disease. These two had spent their days together while I took our other Dachshund, Lumpi (pronounced loompee, German for little rascal) to school with me to do therapy dog work in my deaf education classroom. Now Willie was home alone in his grief, and he suffered extreme separation anxiety - even to the point of injuring his back. We knew we had to get Willie a companion so he wouldn't feel abandoned when Lumpi was out "working," and, of course, it just *had* to be a Dachshund.

As I browsed the Internet for adoptable adult Dachshunds, I came upon the Central Texas Dachshund Rescue website and saw Freckles, a four-month-old double dapple. With his spotted, paint-splashed look he appeared identical to Lumpi. What's more, Freckles was deaf and needed a home that would use sign language with him. My jaw dropped - he was a perfect match!

Then the concern set in. I thought, "We can't adopt a puppy right now - especially not a deaf puppy."

With eleven years of experience teaching deaf students, I am fully aware of their special needs and could not even imagine the work involved with caring for a deaf puppy. Plus, school was still in session, and it was the busiest time of year. No way. I logged off of the computer, and put Freckles out of my mind.

A week later, I just happened to be talking to a co-worker during lunch and told her about Freckles (I guess he wasn't totally out of my mind). She was intrigued and asked me to pull up his picture and bio. After reading about him, she immediately responded, "What the heck are you doing? That's your dog!"

Her comment was all it took. I immediately submitted an application to adopt little Freckles. I shared Freckles' picture and bio with my students and explained that I had applied to adopt him. My students were absolutely fascinated with the idea of a deaf dog. Our discussion became a lesson about rescue organizations, puppy mills, shelters, and why I couldn't just go "purchase" Freckles. The students brainstormed about training a deaf dog and decided it had to be completely visual and tactile.

To call for a deaf dog to come, I would need to have a way to get its attention. One student mentioned using a "tact-aid," a vibro-tactile device some deaf students use. This inspired us to do some research on the Internet, where we found dog collars that produce slight vibrations. My students liked the idea of using a collar similar to a tact-aid with Freckles because I could just "buzz" him to get his attention. It soon became a consensus that if I adopted Freckles, he should be renamed Buzz.

During the application process, I learned that little Freckles came from a flea market in Canton, Texas. He was in a small cage with about ten other Dachshund puppies, all climbing over each other to stay at the top of the pile. The individual who purchased Freckles was smitten with his beautiful blue eyes and unusual coloring. She couldn't stand seeing him in that cage, but after deciding he was too much of a handful, she handed him over to Central Texas Dachshund Rescue. It didn't take Freckles' foster parents long to discover he was deaf, as it is a common trait among double dapple dogs.

Things happened very quickly after that, and Freckles, I mean, *Buzz*, joined our home. What a sweet, little bundle of love he was! At four months of age, he had learned the sign for "no" from his foster mom, but he wasn't yet potty trained and hadn't quite learned that after he went poo, he should step away from it (not in it!).

The next morning, leaving Lumpi and Willie at home, Buzz came to school with me so that I could start working on his potty training and teaching him signs. He was introduced to the entire elementary student body through our broadcasted morning announcements and became an instant celebrity.

Everyone wanted to meet him, and faculty members snatched him up whenever they got the chance.

Buzz accompanied me to school each day for the next several weeks. My students identified with him because he was deaf, just like them, and they took complete ownership of his training. The first sign they taught Buzz was "sit." They also taught him "ball" and "release" (to let go of the ball). Determined that Buzz would learn the command to go potty, when outside my students would surround him, signing "toilet." It was a sight!

Today, Buzz is 18 months old. He responds to over 30 signs/sign language phrases and learns new ones daily. He now alternates his visits to school with Lumpi, who missed his work. Buzz's most popular trick is when he's presented with the sign for "I love you," he does a little jump as if saying, "Yay! You love me!"

Buzz aspires to do pet therapy work, just like his older brother, Lumpi. He is scheduled to take his therapy dog evaluation in a couple of months. We're certain he's ready until he starts displaying the Dachshund trait of unrelenting stubbornness, causing us to question whether or not we should give him a few more months to practice. Dachshunds are certainly known to have minds of their own, and Buzz is no exception.

In the meantime, Buzz continues to share his love with our family and my students. He's just like them in so many ways: eager to learn, thoughtful, loving, and unwilling to let his impairment slow him down.

 *Carolyn Honis*

Wire Hangers in the Closet

There's no need to mince words: my mom and I are Dachshund fanatics. So it should not have come as a surprise to my mom when, out of the blue, she received a call asking if her Dachshund rescue could take on another one.

Except my mom does not run a rescue. Of the three Wieners we had between the two of us, two of them were adopted, but we certainly don't consider ourselves to be a "rescue." Not by any means.

After getting over the initial, "Wow, I must really talk about my dogs a lot if they think I have a rescue!" Momma listened to the little dog's story: A coworker's daughter was doing some cleanup work with her church youth group at a trailer park when they heard something that sounded like running water, coming from within a vacant trailer. The trailer park manager and landlord were summoned, and the water sounds were tracked to the bathroom. They opened the door, and out jumped a scared, hungry, smooth, red Dachshund!

Neighbors were questioned: "Yes, the people who had lived there had owned that dog." "Yes, they had moved out of state a few days ago." "No, it wasn't too surprising that they'd left the dog behind; he had spent many long days just tied up outside and fed scraps."

There were two big questions left unanswered: Who in the world would leave a little dog like this, sealed up in a hot trailer, left to starve? And, more importantly, now that he had been rescued from certain death, what was to be done with the little guy? Thus, the phone call to my mom, and our trio of Wieners had become a foursome.

It was clear that the Doxie, who my mom christened "Red," had some issues. He was afraid of toys and had no idea what a biscuit was. He also wasn't too fond of kibble and had a tough time putting on any weight. You could see his spine, and he was rather drawn up underneath. It was also clear that he had BIG issues with being left alone (no surprise there). Whenever my mom or dad got ready to leave for work in the mornings, he would whimper, cry, bark, and do everything in his power to express his displeasure and beg them to stay.

The long rehabilitation process began. First, the vet check. He tested clean for heartworms and received all of his vaccinations. He had already been neutered. At least *some*one at *some* point had done *some*thing responsible with this poor dog! Mom started adding soft puppy food to his regular kibble diet, which helped Red add a few pounds. Eventually, curiosity got the better of him. After watching his new siblings go crazy for the biscuit tin, he finally joined in the fracas. But perhaps the most epic breakthrough was when my mom called me, all excited because she had found Red chewing on a rope toy! Finally, he had come out of his shell enough to play! He's since become an expert burrower, too.

Today, Red is a happy, healthy, nine-pound Dachshund who bears almost no resemblance to the trembling, little furball that was found in that hot trailer nearly two years ago. He still gets nervous when my mom and dad leave in the morning, especially if one of them is going away overnight and packs a bag, but he's so much better.

We sometimes wonder what those people were thinking by leaving their teeny Weenie behind when they moved, like you would wire hangers in a closet. They could have easily dropped him at a shelter or with a rescue if they didn't want him. We're glad the people who discovered him had the sense to call our "rescue organization," he's been a wonderful addition and we're happy he's here.

 *Holly Benton*

Your Worst Date Couldn't Top This

L ike so many best friends, mine feels it's her job to find me a significant other, so she set me up on a blind date. "Living alone and doing only what you and the dogs want is a bad thing," she lectured, "He likes dogs. He's a nice guy."

Things came together unexpectedly well: liver-sausage-on-cracker appetizers set out on an unbreakable plate, dog hair vacuumed up, dog beds hidden, and only a ½ gallon of Febreze® needed to spruce up the smell. I decided to allow the two best-behaved dogs to be the greeters, while the rest would be introduced at a later time. I also had installed a gate between the hall and the living room to protect the goodies on the coffee table.

When my date Rob arrived, my two four-footed greeters ran to the door as planned. Much to my surprise, he was clean and neat and came complete with flowers and a bottle of wine - maybe this wouldn't be so bad. I was just about to accept the wine when out of the corner of my eye, I spied a Dachshund who had stealthily opened the gate and was headed toward the goodies. In a flash, I jumped the gate and made a dive for the table. Success! I scooped up the tray, only losing one to the hungry Doxie, and then I hurriedly returned to the door, straightening my clothes. Rob had a very quizzical look on his face and said, "Boy, you can really move."

Just as I was about to thank him, I heard the gargling noise a dog makes when it's about to vomit. Yes, indeed, the stealth Dachs did it, right on Rob's shoe. "No problem," I thought, "He loves dogs."

A few paper towels later, we headed into the living room to share the bottle of wine and some treats. Naturally, both greeter dogs felt the need to get up-close and personal with Rob, leaping at his pants legs and slathering his hands with their tongues. After a few minutes, the gentleman began to sneeze and his eyes started to swell. I didn't want to pry, but he had used the whole pile of napkins, so I asked if he was feeling ok. That's when he informed me he was allergic to dogs!

He said our mutual acquaintance had told him I had outdoor dogs, and she was sure they wouldn't bother him. I offered two Benedryl®, and within a half-an-hour, the swelling was gone. He could now see his wine glass, so we were doing fine, right?

I told him our mutual friend had mentioned his love for dogs, and I assumed he had one. The truth was that he had one twenty years ago, but allergies prevented him from getting another. Of course, right when the topic of his allergies came up again, four more dogs breached the gate, and suddenly there were six dogs in his lap, kissing and licking and smelling his private parts!

I thought he was being a good sport: he didn't seem to mind the stain that appeared on his shirt when one of the dogs indiscriminately expressed its anal glands on him, or when his plate was suddenly emptied as another dog swallowed Rob's appetizers. Upon reflection, he was really just so startled he couldn't speak - until his throat began swelling shut and he croaked, "How many are there?"

I told him, "Don't worry, just these six," but he didn't exactly look relieved.

When it was time to go, Rob very politely thanked me for everything and moved to give me a kiss on the cheek. Bad move. "Protector Dachshund" immediately sprang into action and bit his left ankle. Next thing I knew, Rob grabbed his flowers and hurriedly limped down the walkway, blood oozing out of his sock.

I promised I would fax him the rabies certificate and assured him the dogs loved him. I can't imagine why he never called again!

 *Helen LaBuda*

Even an Old Rose Can Blossom

I remember the puppy mill I grew up in as if it were yesterday. The sound of hungry, hurting dogs, barking out in pain either from illness, frustration, or loneliness was deafening. Many even died from a lack of care. Under the circumstances, I often pondered whether *they* were really the lucky ones – we didn't know any better, but for us life was very, very bad.

I was pregnant all of the time: two litters a year for as long as I could remember. I had no exercise, poor food, and no one checking on me or my pups. Until, of course, they were just old enough to take away from me. We were casually separated and I never heard about them again. It was sheer anguish - my poor little ones, the babies I never got the chance to know and love, just gone. I know some were sick and had birth defects, or were traumatized because they were weaned so soon. I can only hope that the "pet store" place I was told they were taken was better than this.

One day I hear a great deal of noise and see an influx of people I had never seen before. I feel their anger and hear lots of shouting. For the first time, my crate is moved, and I'm shocked to see how many others are suffering like me. Some look identical, others different, but we all are neglected and terrified. Life isn't really getting worse, is it?

As the day wears on, similar dogs are grouped into different vans and taken away in separate directions (there were 40 in my group). We ride together down the highway for what seems like hours and are finally dropped off at a rescue. I had heard about my brothers and sisters being sold to other breeders – is that what just happened? Or is this "rescue" place something different?

At first we all just sit there, not knowing what to do or expect. Some dogs can't walk because their toenails are too long, bodies are disfigured, or their feet are splayed out and in pain from the chicken wire we spent our lives standing on. Some are so fearful they become aggressive and have to be moved away from the rest of us. But once we are given good food and clean, cool water, some of us start to relax. Little did we know that the real terror was about to begin.

The day after arriving at the rescue, I am taken away from the group. Imagine my dismay: never out of a cage, sparse interaction with humans, and now I'm lying on a table, surrounded by people in white coats wielding unfamiliar pointy things. What have I ever done to deserve this?

It turns out that the scary people are actually trying to help me: vaccines, a bath, nail trimming, and something I slept through that made it so I would never have to be pregnant again. After a month, I start believing that things are getting better. Regular meals, toys and treats, room to roam, shelter from the weather, and a quiet place to escape to when I need it –this seems much more reasonable that just standing in a cage all day. There's not a lot of personal attention because there are so many of us to attend to, but I'm not sure that's something I want anyway. At least the voices who speak to me seem kind.

Then without warning, my little world is turned upside-down again by a woman who comes into the rescue looking for a pet. I try my best to melt into the wall, but she spots me. Even though I am skinny, frightened, and withdrawn, with no redeeming qualities to speak of, she insists on taking me home with her. This again is really quite scary, but in retrospect I thank God she did.

The new woman names me Charlotte Rose, telling me that like a rose, I'm regal and soft. She gives me my own soft bed in the bedroom, feeds me twice a day, and never forgets to tell me I'm beautiful. In the den I relax on a huge pillow that I share with one or more brothers, who each has his own story: Guthrie = abuse, Frosty = abandonment, Pete = the streets, and Jazz = puppy mill survivor. Jazz and I have especially bonded since we understand each other's pasts so well.

This has been my home for six years now. I try not to look back and instead focus on the different world I have now come to know, full of dogs that are happy, healthy, and loved. Though it took three months for me to wag my tail, and I'm still not comfortable with strangers or vets (who really is?), I'm the happiest dog alive. It's not really the homemade doggie cookies, pig's ears, or pillows (although they're great), it's the human and canine companionship – a glance, a touch, a snuggle. I've never asked for much, and because I've never had much, I appreciate these small, thoughtful gestures all the more.

 *Lucy Butler*

The Grifter

Who had dogs growing up? Not us. Whenever I'd go to my friends' homes, I was pretty much indifferent to their pets. I might say hi. Maybe pet them gingerly and coo a little bit. But kiss them? Let them climb on me or lick my face? No, thank you.

Fast forward to my thirties. Something happens. My friend has two adopted dogs, Jet and Abby. They're a team, these two. They bound up to me, tails wagging, giving me sweet kisses. Can I have a hug? A treat? A bite of your steak, perhaps? I can't stop petting them or cooing to them. They climb all over me, and I'm not at all freaked out. In fact, I feel relaxed. Everything they do makes me laugh. And at some point, it occurs to me: I am in love with these dogs.

I'm starting to like other dogs, too. Dogs I see at the park, in a car, or on walks around the neighborhood. But that doesn't mean I'm getting a dog. I like my life too much the way it is: I go to work, hang out with my friends and boyfriend, take a weekend road trip here and there. Why change it? Why stir up my independent, happy-go-lucky, no-real-responsibilities-except-for-work life? But for some reason one night I decide to look at rescue sites. Just for fun.

I somehow stumble upon the Dachshund Rescue of Houston (DROH) website. "If I were to get a dog," I think, "I would get a Dachshund. But I'm totally not getting a dog. "

And then I see her. Her name is Millie. She doesn't look like any other Dachshund I've seen before. She's black and tan, and her coat looks unruly. She has the funniest, wildest, old-man eyebrows, a little beard, and a crooked front paw. But it's her expression that gets me. Her tongue is sticking out - she looks kind of bored and completely entitled at the same time.

I'm intrigued. I must know more. Millie's a wirehaired Dachshund. Her foster mom describes her as sweet, a little shy, and totally stubborn. She was rescued from the pound and is eight years old, well past her puppy years. DROH knew her chances for survival at the pound weren't great.

I am done. There is no turning back. Right then and there, I fill out the application. A DROH volunteer calls the next day for a phone interview. I've never done this before and I have no idea if what I'm saying is what I'm supposed to say.

It seems to go okay, though, because he decides that I am worthy of a home visit. We schedule it for Saturday. I tell him I'm really interested in Millie and ask if I'll be able to meet her. He explains that I won't meet her until after the home visit. "Fair enough," I think, followed by, "Wait a second, what have I just done?"

Saturday arrives. Shelly, the volunteer home inspector, knocks on my door. With her is a tiny black and tan wirehaired Dachshund. She looks suspiciously like Millie. I figure they've changed their minds and decided to let me meet her after all. Shelly and I sit on the floor, and she starts asking me questions:

"Why do you want a dog?" (I don't know, exactly. I like them?) "Have you ever had a dog?" (No.) "Would you keep my dog inside or outside?" (Inside.) "Would you take my dog on walks?" (Yes!) "Are you willing to pay for vet bills?" (Of course!)

Meanwhile, Millie is checking me out, sniffing and licking my hand. Satisfied that I've been properly attentive, she eyes my sofa and leaps onto it. She seems pretty comfortable. She also seems to know something is up.

"So," Shelly asks, "Have you looked at the pictures on the site? Is there a particular dog you're interested in?"

I look at her, confused. "I want Millie," I say. "Isn't that why you brought her here?"

As it turns out, Millie's foster mom is allergic to her, so Shelly is taking her to another foster home today. But Millie never makes it to her new foster home because looking at her on my sofa, it is so obvious. She is already home.

Five years on and I can't really remember my life before Millie. Of course, I remember events, people, and places, but I can't remember how I felt. What I feel now was definitely not there before, and I didn't even know it. How on earth did I go over 30 years without a dog? How could I know that this little, 12-pound creature I'd never met before would make me laugh every day? That I'd be a slave to her demands for belly rubs, walks, and treats? That she'd bring me so much joy, so much love, so much more than words can describe?

My husband Walt, who was my boyfriend when I adopted Millie, is convinced she's a grifter. "Look at her," he says, as Millie burrows beneath our bed covers. "She was in the pound, and now she's sleeping in our bed every night. She tricked the DROH people into bringing her to your house that day. She totally knew what she was doing."

I have to agree. Millie knew what she was doing. She knew she had to find me because she knew I needed her. She knew all of this before I did. Dachshunds are smart that way.

 *Melissa Quiroz Campbell*

A Long Pause...

The General Dachshund: Before I adopted Barkley, he was afraid of everything and everyone. He found common things like paper bags, wind, and fire hydrants terrifying. Oddly enough, Barkley chose me as his human, a general contractor who plays with very loud tools all day. Now he's gotten over his fear *and* taken to construction! Barkley "helps" me in my workshop and is enamored with big, noisy tools like grinders, table saws, welders, and drills. I'm afraid he's going to start stealing my clients. – *Gary Green*

The Snappy Dresser: 15-year-old Chad is normally shy and scared, but he gets over his fears very quickly at the prospect of dressing up. We discovered this behavior one day when I brought home some children's clothing to alter and turn into doggie clothes. Chad spotted me holding up a sweater, came galloping across the room, ducked his head, and *zoom*, he had it on! Chad is Mr. GQ in this house and no other dog is allowed that place of honor. -*Kathleen Hotchkiss*

Vinnie Joins our Mob

O ur local Humane Society called and asked if I, as a representative of Florida Dachshund Rescue (FLDR), could take in a senior, red, mini-Dachshund. He was a stray with no identification, and after a week in the shelter no one had shown up to claim him. Naturally I rushed over to get him.

Vinnie was literally skin and bones - I could count his vertebrae and ribs, and he felt very frail in my arms. I named him Vinnie because it rhymed with "skinny-mini," which is exactly what he was. He was desperately in need of vet care and nourishment for both his body and soul. I whisked him off to the vet for neutering, vaccinations, and a complete dental.

Vinnie had no upper or lower front teeth, and he lost a few more during his dental. The missing teeth give him comical expressions as his lips get hung up on his unusually large incisors. This has earned him the nickname "Vinnie the Lip." His tongue also sticks out in front as if he's giving a big ol' raspberry.

Poor Vinster has also been diagnosed with a high-grade heart murmur. So far it's not affecting the quality of his life - he's a spunky little guy - but the vet suspects he'll eventually need to be put on heart medication.

Because he had no body fat, Vinnie was always cold. At night I wrapped his shivering body in a blanket, put him in bed with me, and curled my body around him to keep him warm. In time, a high-quality diet helped him put on weight and he's not quite so cold now.

All this body contact bonded us quickly. Vinnie was supposed to be a foster, but after only a few days with him I knew he was meant to stay right here with me and my other four Dachshunds. Even now, almost two years later, Vinnie smothers me with thank-you kisses after every meal. I always kiss him back, and say, "You're welcome." The sweetest Doxie I've ever met, Vinnie may have a "boo-boo" heart, but it is 100% full of love.

 *Lorrie Corsetti*

The Ripple Effect

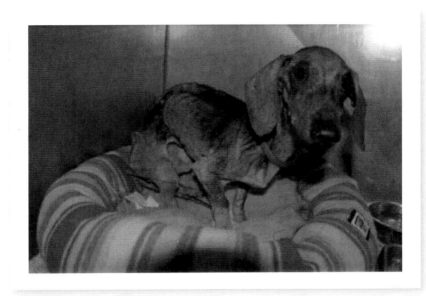

The saying goes, *"The world is like a stone being thrown into a pond; that one stone causes ripples throughout the pond's world that echo back and forth between its banks."*

I am the stone. It all began last spring when a caring person found me lying beside a busy road and, figuratively, threw me into the pond's world of rescue. The ripples caused have been many. Almost 400 people have contributed to my care, from nine countries outside the United States, and from 38 states within. Can you just imagine that one little six-pound dog could cause such a ripple and touch so many hearts? One of the contributors, who didn't even have a job, and probably not enough money to care for himself, sent $1.00 to help care for me. Such are the ripples caused by caring for another living being.

My name now is Joan of Arc. I am so named because I am a fighter. I weigh only eight-and-a-half pounds, about half what I should weigh. I have very little hair, almost every bone in my body is visible through my skin, I can barely stand for more than a few minutes at a time, but I fight on just to live.

As you know, my rescue story begins beside a road. Traffic sped by me on all sides. I was spent, dehydrated, too weak to move, and scared like I had never been before. The manager of a local animal shelter made it her mission to see I received the care I so desperately needed by contacting All Texas Dachshund Rescue (ATDR), who gladly took me in. Their contributors and volunteers have seen to it that I have the most comfortable beds in which to lie and the best food to eat. Their vet said I was the worst case of emaciation he had ever seen in a living dog and that it was almost unbelievable how I had no signs of illness, renal failure, or heartworms.

My foster mom, Cindy, called and visited 20 pharmacy companies before she finally found one that would compound a special chicken-flavored dose of the medicine I need to keep me alive. Slowly, I discovered other reasons to live: boiled chicken, duck and potato dog food, even cherry vanilla yogurt! This trying-to-put-weight-on-me business is just plain fun! I'm also noticing other fun things around me, like birds and dogs. My foster mom continues to nurse and care for me, rejoicing with every tiny sign of progress I make: taking a few more steps, eating all my food, noticing and interacting with the things around me, and best of all, kissing and cuddling.

The ripples I caused in the pond of rescue have become ripples in so many personal ponds – my foster mom, the kind folks at ATDR, those who have contributed time and money to my care - the ripples continue to echo between the banks of each of their ponds. People's lives are touched by my story, and every day I appreciate the benefits these ripples bring me. The best thing I can do for the world of rescue is to keep the ripples going by continuing to fight for my life. But hey, like Joan of Arc, a fighter I am.

 *Tina Brandon*

Twinkle, Twinkle, Cindy Lou

D ickens said it so clearly, "It was the best of times; it was the worst of times."

We were in the middle of selling our home of thirty years, and moving was physically and emotionally exhausting. At the end of one particularly long day, I visited the Diamond Dachshund Rescue of Texas (DDRT) website. The Doxies are so cute, and the happy endings are so uplifting that I often go there when my spirit needs a boost. Already we had been twice blessed with two wonderful adopted Dachshunds. Adopting another was something we were not even considering. What drew me to view the available dogs on the website that day we'll leave to fate.

There she was: a little thing, hair a mess, eyes full of hope. Cindy Lou really wasn't much to look at, but those eyes got me. She looked into my soul and was forever locked inside my heart. As hard as I tried, I could not keep from going back to her picture over and over.

Cindy Lou came into our life at what some would call the most inopportune time. Boxes everywhere, movers coming, repair people going, and here we had this fragile, little girl. I feared something would happen to her with all that commotion.

My solution was simple. She must be kept close, snuggled next to my heart to keep her safe. Cindy Lou spent the first two weeks as our newest family member tucked into a baby sling. Her daddy was convinced she would never learn to walk among us, but my instincts were guiding me, and she flourished.

After all, her little life had not been so easy. Starved almost to death in a puppy mill, she had been ignored and didn't know the feeling of love and a full tummy. With her new mommy, she was getting way more than just the nutrition she desperately needed. She was getting all my love.

For four years my tiny angel filled my heart and my life. She brought me smiles and laughter at some of my lowest points. The eyes that drew me in are etched in my memory, but Cindy Lou left us way too soon.

I never imagined when I awoke that Saturday morning it would be the last we spent together. As was our custom, I let her out first thing. Always fearful of snakes, I followed her everywhere when she was outside. Why did I walk up the steps first this time? I turned at the top of the steps just in time to see her poke that little nose under a potted plant. A yelp, and then an all-too-familiar noise followed. A rattlesnake had bitten Cindy Lou. We rushed her to the vet, who hospitalized her and began treatment immediately. She tried so hard for five days, but her little body just gave out and she slipped into forever sleep.

Just as Dickens said, it's the best of times and the worst of times. My Cindy Lou is gone from Earth, but she's not gone from my life. There is a star that is not often out when I walk onto the deck and turn my eyes toward the heavens. Before long, as I begin to talk, the star emerges. The more I talk, the brighter it shines and twinkles. I know it's my Cindy Lou. I can no longer hold her, feel her nose next to my cheek, or kiss her little face, but God has blessed me with a star to gaze upon before I lay my head each night.

 *Patti Oestreich*

Multiple Dachshund Syndrome (MDS)

When I was young, my cousins owned a Dachshund. I always thought they were saying "Datsun," so I spent many years thinking that was the name of the breed. The dog barked incessantly, always seemed to be peeing whether he was marking or just excited, and was extremely food aggressive.

I spent 40 years with the attitude that I would NEVER own one of those ankle-biters. But despite our preventative efforts, my husband, Chris, and I came down with a bad case of MDS...

My sister had just lost her Dalmatian of 10 years, who died right on the floor in front of her. She believed that getting a new puppy would help her overcome her tremendous grief, so she combed every shelter in the Seattle area looking for the right dog - knowing that when she found it she would know, because it would choose her.

After several weeks of hunting, she went down to visit our mother in Portland who joined her in checking out local shelters, but still no dog "chose" her. Her last stop was a no-kill shelter about a ½ mile from our mother's house. They went in, loved all the dogs, but yet again came out empty-handed.

Just as they were getting in the car to leave, they met a lady dropping off a tiny puppy she had just captured on a busy, four-lane roadway. The puppy wasn't more than eight weeks old, and because of its age, it was difficult to tell the breed or gender. Regardless, that little thing picked my sister to be its mommy before the lady ever entered the shelter. My sister explained her search, and the lady agreed to give her the puppy. Long story short, the puppy never made it in to the shelter, but instead went home with my sister.

Two days later, back in Seattle, my sister suddenly required major emergency surgery. My husband and I cared for the puppy while she recovered for a week, but we still couldn't figure out its breed. We saw a little "puff" between its legs and naturally assumed it was a boy, and since my sister hadn't gotten around to naming him yet, we decided to call him O'Malley.

That was a tough week. We already owned two eight-year-old Whippets who wanted nothing more than to play with O'Malley. We had to constantly supervise them and give everyone separate feedings and visits outside to potty. We also had to put a dog bed in the middle of *our* bed because we were afraid the tiny thing would try to jump up or down to get to us, and we didn't have the heart to leave it crying in the kennel.

The week finally ended, and we returned O'Malley to my sister, believing the puppy would help her emotionally during her recovery. Two days later my sister called us crying, saying that she didn't know what she was thinking and could not possibly take on raising a new puppy in her condition. We immediately told her not to worry - we had grown so attached in that short, tiring week that we would take O'Malley and add him to our pack.

On our first trip to the vet for a check-up and vaccines we got more information than we could have imagined. First, O'Malley was *not* a boy (as you may have guessed). *Her* "puff" was actually her lady-business. But that was nothing compared to the *real* shocker: the puppy was a Dachshund! She was so chubby and short, how could she be a Dachshund?

Hmmm, now what to do? Neither Chris nor I had ever liked Dachshunds and definitely didn't think we'd EVER own one. We looked at each other and kind of laughed and said, "Well, I guess we have one of those ankle-biters now."

Since O'Malley was a "she," we renamed her Sadie and bought her a new set of tags. We took her back home and set the house up for our baby. Having no children ourselves, she became our obsession. Can you believe it? We were in *love* with a Datsun!

I had never seen a puppy with such attitude. Sadie truly believed she was tough enough to take on anything, including her daddy. She constantly wrestled with him and nibbled on him, making these strange, gurgling, tongue-twisting noises that had us rolling on the floor, laughing. I had never heard sounds like that coming from any animal - it was more "talking" than barking.

As Sadie began to elongate (but not really get any taller), it became apparent that the vet was right, she was a Dachshund, and we were miraculously converted. I'm now obsessed with Doxies, looking at them online all the time, and Chris just loves to play with her.

Ironically, we moved back down to Portland from Seattle shortly after Sadie joined our family, putting Sadie back in her hometown. Since my husband works and I stay home, her connection with me grew stronger and stronger, and she soon became somewhat of a momma's girl. Daddy was jealous and decided he needed his own Datsun.

On Petfinder we came across Oregon Dachshund Rescue, which had a two-year-old male we liked. Upon calling we found that he was not yet ready for adoption, but they said they had a male named Elvis we just had to meet.

Talk about total opposites! Elvis is shy and sad-looking, with *very* short legs, and a foot stool-shaped body. Sadie is outgoing, quite tall now, and has a physique that resembles an otter.

Elvis has a variety of specialty moves, including the kick-punch, which he immediately demonstrated to my husband. For such a short guy, he could jump up my husband's leg and lunge at him, nearly knocking him back. He continued this until my husband picked him up, and then he made my husband the recipient of his kisses. Apparently this was the first time Elvis had kissed anyone since he'd been rescued, which was all my husband needed to hear – he now had a Datsun of his own, or so he thought.

Elvis came to be known as Jackson. After coming home with us that night, things didn't go quite as my husband had planned. Any Dachshund lover knows that they pick us just as much as we pick them, and although my husband chose Jackson, Jackson had other ideas... we now had a mommy's *boy*!

Both Doxies love my husband tremendously, playing with him in ways they don't with me, but they always want to sleep with me and follow me around. My husband is *convinced* that Doxie number three will become a daddy's boy. I guess with our next rescue we'll find out...

Have you heard of MDS (Multiple Dachshund Syndrome)? Do you have it yourself? Our understanding is that there is only one cure... more Datsuns!

 *Leslie and Chris Ireland*

Editor's Follow Up: Leslie and Chris' Multiple Dachshund Syndrome has become more serious, and it appears that no amount of Dachshunds can cure them. As this book was going to print, they wrote me to say that they rescued *another* Doxie named Oliver, a blue dapple male. They also decided that once their aging Whippets go on "the big run through a field," they will acquire four more Doxies (two Dachshunds for each Whippet – they're only half the size). Will Leslie and Chris survive? Friends and family ask that you please keep them in your thoughts as they struggle to avoid the inevitable - turning into Dachshunds, themselves. *-KD*

Katrina's Little Angel

Angel was rescued by a group of volunteers that traveled from Texas to Louisiana many times during the aftermath of Hurricane Katrina. On one of the search-and-rescue trips, the volunteers discovered a puppy mill in an old out-building on an abandoned property. The storm had flooded the property and reached as high as seven feet inside the building. Crates were stacked from floor to ceiling, and unfortunately everyone below the waterline had drowned.

Angel and her brother Dominick were in one of the top crates. When the water receded, the crates shifted and theirs fell to the ground. Dominick got lucky and landed on his sister, who broke his fall. This left Angel with a traumatic back injury, and days without food or water made the pair so weak that when rescuers arrived, they thought Angel and Dominick were dead. Their survival could only have been a miracle!

The dogs were brought to safety at a makeshift shelter in Lafayette, LA, where workers determined that Angel's injury would, indeed, require medical attention. Volunteers transported the pair to Beaumont, TX, where they were evaluated by a vet. A kind couple then drove them to Houston, where they spent the night with a volunteer. The next day, Dominick was taken to San Antonio to reside in foster care with Diamond Dachshund Rescue while Angel continued on to a surgeon in Austin and was cared for by All Texas Dachshund Rescue. She underwent extensive spinal surgery the following morning.

This young, beautiful, black-and-tan piebald "angel" touched the hearts of everyone she met. Angel's Houston transport volunteer was so taken by her that she offered to foster Angel through her rehabilitation. She recovered well but needed lots of therapy and acupuncture following her surgery. After months of hard work and expensive therapy, Angel wiggled her way into her foster mom's heart. Now Angel's "forever" mom, she can't imagine life without her.

While Hurricane Katrina devastated many areas of the South, it actually may have saved Angel and Dominick's lives. Had it not struck, they would most likely still be stuck in a cage at that puppy mill. Angel's strength and will to survive is a testament to all of the tireless volunteers who helped during Hurricane Katrina. Their work has not gone unnoticed, especially by two little dogs whose lives would have been lost if not for their selfless efforts.

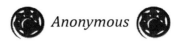 *Anonymous*

A Long Pause...

Teeth, Who Needs 'em? Charlie had severe periodontal disease: His breath was so foul it could be smelled across the room, and some of the teeth were so rotten they literally crumbled out of his mouth. The only cure for the poor guy was to have all of his teeth extracted. When I got him, he drooled like a St. Bernard, and his tongue slipped out the side of his mouth. Quickly he adjusted to his lack of teeth, the drooling stopped, and his breath got better. He now gives sweet-smelling sideways kisses! -*Lorrie Corsetti*

Two Is Better than One: If we didn't have two, Linux and Rosie couldn't chase each other around the house or trade dog bowls during meals. Linux couldn't watch while Rosie shreds paper towels and rips up tennis balls, and Rosie couldn't enjoy witnessing Linux sneak into our treat cabinet. They couldn't snuggle and cuddle together or "protect" each other from the vet. One lonely Doxie? What fun would that be? TWO is the magic number! - *Anonymous*

Frank Takes a Dip

Frank Weenie is one of the happiest, friendliest, most devoted dogs you can imagine. He loves to run in the backyard, play fetch with his stuffed duck, go on car rides, play games with his cousins Max and Shocko, nap, help his Dad grill in the backyard, and go on walks at the park. There is one thing, though, that Frank does not like - water. Frank hates water. Loathes it. Does anything and everything he can to avoid it. On walks, Frank insists on crossing the street at least two houses ahead of any yard sprinklers, and he can squeeze through the narrowest path in order to avoid touching a puddle of water. On rainy mornings Frank often fakes out his mom, making her think he went potty outside, only to sneak back in and leave a present on nice dry carpet. He truly hates water.

One day Frank went to a party with his mom and dad. This was no ordinary party - it was a Dachshund rescue party! There were dozens of Dachshunds and volunteers enjoying lots of loud barks, runs around the house, games, and fun. Frank was having a blast playing chase until he went outside and made a horrifying discovery: there was a pool.

Frank's mom and dad decided to hop in the pool since it was a hot Texas Saturday, but Frank stayed on the patio at a safe distance from the water. A few other volunteers joined in, and two Dachshunds took dips, too. Frank saw what was going on and decided to take a closer look at the pool. He very slowly came to the edge, and then quickly retreated to safer ground. A few minutes later he approached the edge again, trying to see what all the fuss was about. Again he scurried away from the pool's edge. At this point his mom, dad, and the other volunteers had noticed Frank's interest in the water and began to chant, "Go Frank, go Frank, go Frank!" Frank quickly realized he had a choice to make: he would have to run and hide or prove to everyone that he was not afraid of the water.

Again approaching the edge of the pool, Frank took one look down at the water and decided it was time to go for it. Frank *dove* headfirst into the water and came up in his dad's arms. Next he swam over to his mom, kicking and splashing along the way. He then turned around, swam to the edge, and hopped out. The crowd went wild, clapping and cheering Frank on for being so brave. Frank strutted around the party for the rest of the day with his chest out and head held high. His dad coined him the Michael Phelps of Dachshunds.

The next day Frank's mom and dad take him for a walk. As they turn a corner, they see a neighbor's sprinkler splashing onto the sidewalk. This is the true test. Will Frank now play in puddles and sprinklers? Will he enjoy puppy baths? Will he go swimming again? Nope! Frank hits the brakes and demands that they cross the street. "Once a Dachshund always a Dachshund," stubborn Frank is back to his old self.

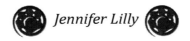 *Jennifer Lilly*

Change of Heart

I n my mind, Dachshunds are pushy, bossy, and loud, and the "cute factor" just isn't there for me.

Then I saw Oscar's photo on the Cowlitz County rescue site. He was missing most of his hair due to a flea allergy, but his beautiful, big, brown eyes looked so very sad and lonely. I had no intention of adopting a dog as we already had two, so what was the harm in inquiring, right? Well, I'm still not sure what happened, but one day I found myself driving the two hours back home from the Cowlitz County rescue with a Dachshund, of all things.

The first week or so Oscar was the perfect dog. He lived to chase balls until he was too tired to run anymore. He was quiet, nice to the other dogs, and happy as long as his ball was within grabbing distance. Gradually things changed, though. Oscar began quietly restructuring the pecking order in the household. If he felt there was too much rambunctious play with the other dogs, he would bring order to chaos. He understood that everybody slept in our room, but *he* slept in our bed. He believed dinner should be at a certain time, after ball time, of course, so he made sure everyone was in their places for dinner, and not wandering willy-nilly about the kitchen. Oscar became the enforcer, so we called him "Boss Man."

He loved his canine companions, but his huge heart was full of love for all of his family, including us humans. He taught me that Dachsunds give their hearts, wholly, fully, and without reservation. Even though Boss Man is gone now, we will never be without a Doxie again!

 *Cate Mayer*

Don't Read This While You're Eating

One day a friend introduced me to Petfinder.com, where she was looking for a new dog. I was fascinated that they had over 300,000 homeless pets posted, and was equally taken by the profile of a paralyzed Dachshund named Skippy. I had never seen a dog in a wheelchair before, and for days felt compelled to return to his profile, rereading it over and over again. I was not in the market for another dog, (I already had a Yorkie), but before I knew it I was emailing the rescue group to adopt Skippy.

I found out that Skippy had been in foster care for three years - he must have been waiting for me! I filled out an application and we began to make travel arrangements. Skippy was in Illinois, and I am in Georgia, so we met halfway in Tennessee.

The first few days with Skippy were a disaster. I had not been completely informed about Skippy's toileting abilities (or lack thereof). He was bladder and bowel incontinent and left a mess wherever he went. I kept him in the guest bathroom at night and while I was at work because the hard floor was easier to clean. Regardless, I was constantly cleaning the carpet, bathing him, and doing laundry. On top of everything, Skippy was completely withdrawn. He wouldn't make eye contact and couldn't care less that I was in the room. Needless to say I was very disheartened and worried that I had made a terrible mistake.

I tried doggie diapers and belly bands, but because Skippy dragged himself around, he easily got right out of them (he doesn't use the cart at home). My next thought was to put him in a baby "onesie" to hold things together, but that didn't work either. Finally, I put him in a doggie harness and pinned the belly wrap to it with old-fashioned diaper pins. It worked! (Well, for pee, anyway. Poop still just happened, but it was relatively easy to clean up.)

The work would have been worth it if I thought Skippy was happy, but he just had a blank look on his face and no life in his eyes. He never looked at me, and he never played. Then one day while I was sitting on the floor with Skippy, he looked into my eyes. After what seemed like forever, he sort of shook his head, and the veil was lifted! It was as though he suddenly realized that he was home and that I was his forever mommy. He even licked my face!

We were making progress on the emotional front but the potty issues were still overwhelming. I had heard the term "expressing the bladder" but didn't know what that involved. Finally finding some instructions online, I tried it – squeezing Skippy as I supported him over a pee pad. I was rewarded with a little bit of pee!

For days I thought I was doing the best I could until one night Skippy was being very wiggly, and I really squeezed him hard. He peed for five minutes and then seemed so relieved. I guess I had just been too timid to put enough pressure on him to fully empty his bladder.

Now that I know what I am doing, my carpets are a lot cleaner. Eventually, I taught him how to stand politely on the toilet seat, and I express his pee right into the toilet and flush it away. No more stinky pee pads!

About a year later, Skippy and I were vacationing at a hotel with my niece and nephew. My two-year-old niece was working on potty training. I noticed Skippy was about to poop, and I thought it would be a great incentive for my niece if she could see that Skippy went poop in the potty (I had never tried it with Skippy before). I grabbed Skippy and held him over the toilet. Sure enough, he pooped right into the potty! I began to wonder if I could control when and where Skippy went poop, just as I did with his pee. In no time at all, I learned how to express his poop, too! Woo-hoo!

Mastering Skippy's bladder and bowels completely changed my life. Now I can take Skippy anywhere with no fear that he will have a messy accident. In many ways Skippy is now my easy dog. I never have to take him out into the rain or snow to go potty - we just go down the hall to the bathroom!

 *Angela Johnston*

Better than Men

One day, a lovely, chocolate and tan, dapple, long-haired Dachshund named Spirit arrived at the vet. The owner said she had suddenly noticed this two-year-old dog was blind. She had just sold his littermate who served as his seeing-eye dog, and she wanted him to be put to sleep. Well, the vet had more ethics than the owner, and he contacted All Texas Dachshund Rescue (ATDR). I fostered him while we begged the previous owner to find out if we could reunite him with his seeing-eye littermate (I would gladly have *paid* for the dog), but she refused to even try. While we knew Spirit would not be the same without his companion, we were still certain we could give him a wonderful life.

Suddenly alone and thrust in a totally new life, Spirit was frightened beyond belief. He was totally scared of men and never warmed up to my ex (I guess he was smarter than I was, huh?). For over a year, he lived on a foot stool under my computer desk during the day and at the far edge of the bed by my feet at night. As soon as I got smart and removed the ex from my life, Spirit glowed! He became one of the happiest dogs I have known.

Since becoming single, Spirit has decided he is to be my main man. Normally, he still sleeps down at my feet, but each night after I've been out on a date, he will sleep next to me on my pillow, as if to remind me that *he* is all I need!

There have been many days when I almost forget that Spirit is blind, as I could swear that he is looking at something. He flies out the doggie door to bark at the dogs next door with the rest of the pack. He is as happy and normal as a dog can be, and has enriched my life more than the ex ever could have.

 *Zandra Clay*

Cocoa's Not Just for Christmastime

It was about 6:00, and Barbara was putting the finishing touches on her makeup before heading out the door to attend the annual Christmas party for the rescue group she'd founded to save Dachshunds.

Just then the call came in. 33 Dachshunds seized from a backyard breeder in Corpus Christi, Texas, had all been adopted out, except one. Paralyzed, she sat in pain, watching each of her siblings get adopted, hoping someone would help her. No one gave her a second look once they found out she was paralyzed; no one wanted to care for an incontinent dog. And now she was to be put down in the morning. Would the rescue please, please take this dog?

The party would go on without Barbara, the guests would certainly understand. She immediately decided to make the two-and-a-half hour drive, taking her friend Linda with her, to pick up little Cocoa.

Cocoa was a beautiful chocolate and tan, tiny, 10-pound girl, still full of milk from her last litter. But wait a minute, wasn't she paralyzed? And the breeder had bred her anyway? Barbara just shook her head in disgust and gathered up the little bundle wrapped in an old towel. As they headed back toward Austin, her big, brown eyes pierced Barbara's heart as if to say, "Thank you for your kindness."

She didn't cry, she didn't whimper, but Barbara knew she must be in pain. After all, her back injury could have been a recent occurrence. And what was that odor?

"Stop the car a minute, Linda, while I check under this towel. I think she's had an accident."

When Barbara opened the towel, she gasped in horror. Where there should have been a leg, there was just a foul-smelling, gangrenous mess. Cocoa's foot had been scraping against the concrete floor as she dragged herself around her pen caring for her pups - bone was exposed, tendons were severed, and the open wound was festering! It brought tears to Barbara's eyes.

"Don't worry, baby, I'll take care of you from now on," she told the poor, frightened animal.

Clearly, little Cocoa was long overdue for some medical attention, so upon reaching Austin, they headed straight for the emergency clinic. The on-call vet took one look at the injured leg and knew she'd need to see the specialist and have her leg removed. But as it turns out, both the specialist and Cocoa's new foster Mom were determined to save that leg. They started treatments but nothing seemed to help - too much tissue had been destroyed. Weeks later, a last ditch effort was attempted: They wrapped Cocoa's leg in a sugar poultice. The poultice would help draw out the infection and keep the wound moist, while the sugar would inhibit the growth of bacteria. After a while, it started to work. There was light at the end of the tunnel finally, and they knew the leg would be saved.

Her leg was healing, but Cocoa Puff still had other issues to surmount. Since she'd had no control of her bowels or bladder for some time, she had been pushing her feces out of her way with her snout, dragging the top of her nose repeatedly across the hard cement floor of her cage. Not only had the cement cut her, the feces had also burned her nose. Her coat was very thin and her eyelashes were missing from malnutrition; it took months of proper food before hair returned to her underside. But most of all, she'd need rehabilitation for her back and her spirit. She now had to learn to be someone's beloved pet.

Throughout the winter, Cocoa Puff went to a veterinary therapist to work on a balance board and have sessions on the underwater treadmill. Fortunately it seemed that Cocoa Puff's feeling and movement had returned to her legs, even though her brain still couldn't receive signals from her bladder or control the muscles to her bathroom functioning. That spring Barbara started taking Cocoa Puff swimming with her, tickling her sides to get her to kick her legs. She grew stronger and stronger, yet still spent her days trying to drag herself across Barbara's slippery floors.

Meanwhile, her personality blossomed, and she grew into a happy little girl, barking excitedly whenever someone approached her, as if to say, "Pick me up! Pick me up!" She was on her rescue group's website, in the hope that someday, a forever home would be found for her.

It turned out that forever home was me! One day in the middle of summer, Cocoa Puff's mischievous face caught my eye on a website, and I quickly adopted her. My home was a good fit, and she soon discovered that our carpeting provides enough traction for her to be able to do her own version of what I like to call "walkies." On longer walks, she rides in her stroller, much to the amusement of passersby who always smile and point at the lucky little princess getting a free ride!

She's a protective guard dog, a bothersome sister to her Dachshund brothers, a funny friend to me, and a survivor. She goes nuts when she sees Barbara, smothering her in Cocoa Puff kisses. I'm certain she remembers all that Barbara did for her, not the least of which is all the love Barbara gave.

 *Melinda Wharton*

Wilbur's Jell-O® Distribution Service

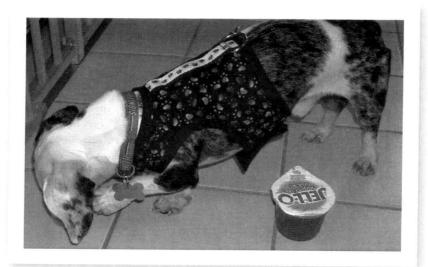

All the dogs in our house know Tuesday is the night we clean out the fridge in preparation for garbage day. As soon as the trash can appears and I block the fridge door open, they are all on scene, working the area for anything that might hit the floor by accident. They patiently wait for the tidbits of dried vegetables, old lettuce, and cherry tomatoes that miss the trash can as they fly through the air.

No dogs were small enough to actually climb in and clean off the shelves until Mr. Wilbur came along. He's a sneaky little Double Dapple who is very inquisitive and doesn't miss anything that relates to food.

I decided to go for the gold this week and wash down all the fridge walls, too, so I took out all the top shelves thinking I had removed all the food. Just as I was about to begin, I heard the washer out of balance in the basement, so figuring it was safe to leave the door open, I sprinted down the stairs to rebalance the load.

Job completed and new load in the machine, I went back to the kitchen to finish the fridge. As I reentered the room, I saw everyone huddled around Wilbur, staring adoringly at him. It turns out he noticed a six-pack of Jell-O in the back of the fridge, climbed in, and pulled out the treasure.

There Wilbur stood, in the middle of the kitchen, removing the foil tops from each container and then passing them out like an ice cream truck driver passes out ice cream. Delilah and Bully were already enjoying their treats while my other two Doxies waited patiently in line. For a second I thought that Wilbur was going to turn around and ask them for twenty-five cents!

I must admit, I was fascinated. I just stood and watched my little Wilbur serve his customers. Sadly for the last two dogs, I had to intervene, and with that Wilbur's illegal Jello® distribution service was busted.

Moral of the story: Never underestimate a Dachshund's determination when it comes to Jell-O®!

 *Helen LaBuda*

Oregon Dachshund (and Human) Rescue

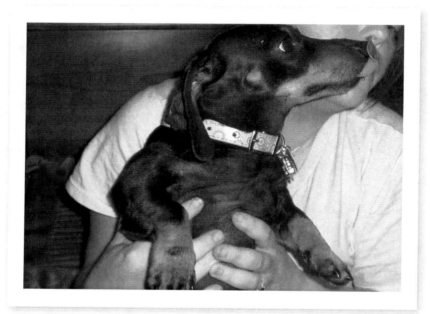

My husband and I were given a Dachshund and told it was abused and homeless. She was a doll and so we took her in. Everything was fine until a week after we licensed her. A knock at the door revealed a police officer, asking about our new dog. We were heartbroken and shocked to find out that she apparently had owners who were looking for her. Despite my daughter's tears, he apologized and took her away.

I searched online forever trying to find another Dachshund that would suit our family. Money was an issue, as I was laid-off and had already spent too much on the dog we were told was homeless. We had to find one we could afford. When I finally discovered Oregon Dachshund Rescue's website, I was thrilled. They helped us through the adoption process and even gave us a payment plan. The minute we met Lucy, the dog they recommended to us, we were in love.

Before we adopted Lucy, I was depressed about the fact that at 29, I had been diagnosed with Multiple Sclerosis and was also unable to make ends meet. Since she came to live with us, I have traded staying depressed in my room all day with family trips to the park to take Lucy out. Taking her everywhere with me gives me the strength to face each day's challenges. We have a bond that I have never before experienced with an animal - she talks to me with her unique little grunts, and snuggles with me when I need her. Lucy even wears a Multiple Sclerosis awareness tag on her collar for me!

I'm not sure if people realize how important the work is that animal rescuers do. They take in dogs that sometimes have significant needs and spare no time nor expense in rehabilitating them. I'm grateful that the kind folks at Oregon Dachshund Rescue saved Lucy. What they may not know is that they rescued me, too! Hmmm… Maybe they should change the name to Oregon Dachshund and Human Rescue…

 *Corinne Winters*

A Priceless Bentley

One hot, summer day in Oregon, my boss came into town from Chicago for some meetings. It turned out Tom had more on his agenda than just work, though. Back home, he was very involved with animal rescue, and so he wanted to check out Oregon's animal shelters while he was here. I soon found out there was a third item on his agenda, too - apparently, Tom thought that it was time for my husband and me to get a dog!

Tom emailed me a picture of a wonderful Dachshund from the Oregon Dachshund Rescue website. I was apprehensive because our cat Juno had been an "only animal" for 15 years.

I didn't know how she would react to another animal in our home, but knew my husband was excited to get a dog. The write-up portrayed Bentley as a Dachshund that did not have a hard life and just needed a new place to live. He seemed like a perfect fit, and his picture was adorable - just sitting on a couch, waiting for us to go get him. I figured we should give it a try.

When we called the rescue to ask about Bentley, they told us that the write-up was wrong, and that Bentley was badly abused, had tons of fleas, and was just coming out of a very bad neuter. We were disappointed, but decided to meet Bentley anyway. Upon being introduced, we realized that the write-up may not have been so far off - Bentley just needed an amazing, new life (with us), so we took him home. What a difference a year makes! He has grown into the most adorable Dachshund around. He loves his new life and his buddy Juno, and we all love him right back.

I wasn't really planning on getting a dog that hot, summer day, but I'm glad that Tom was planning one for me. As my boss, I guess he could have given me a raise instead, but the love and joy Bentley has brought to our home is priceless!

 *Doug and Franny Williams*

Finders, Keepers!

Alittle over a year ago I was searching the web for a Dachshund puppy for my mom. I came across the Dachshund Adoption, Rescue, and Education (DARE) website, and even though I quickly realized it was not a puppy site, I continued to look at all the Dachshunds because if you love them you just can't help it. I clicked around and came across the "urgent needs" Dachshunds and my heart began to ache. There I saw Patrick, the most beautiful, sweet-faced boy, with big, soulful, brown eyes, and I was in love.

I forgot all about my mom and why I was on the computer to begin with. Patrick's story just broke my heart. He had been left, unable to move, floating in a canal, and was rescued by an angel. He was taken for back surgery, which grabbed my attention because I've had three back surgeries myself. I knew just how much pain he was in and how much recovery he would need. Something told me we need that little guy in our life. When I approached my husband about it, though, he said, "Are you crazy? We already have two good dogs. We don't need any more."

Regardless, I kept thinking about Patrick and how he would probably have a hard time getting adopted. The thought of him not having a forever home was unbearable, so I contacted his foster mom, Ms. Sharon, and asked how he was. Ms. Sharon was very kind and we began emailing back and forth. Our vet then reassured us that it was possible Patrick could recover, and that helped me to convince my husband we needed him.

The adoption process seemed to take forever, but we finally got our new boy. Since then, Patrick has flourished. He loves the car and plays so cute with his toys and with his little brother Copper. His back has been just fine, and he is running and jumping like he never had a problem – a far cry from the poor dog that was found floating in a canal.

I never did find my mom that perfect pup, but at least I still gave one a home – with me!

 *Tammy Quinton-Olsson*

Unsolved Mysteries

My husband and I started the day with our morning ritual: walking our five dogs down to the river. It was a beautiful spring morning, and we felt blessed to live on 20 acres of Ozark natural beauty along the banks of the White River with our wonderful dogs: Molly (the grande dame Boxer), Ruby and Shiloh (Labs), and Lulu and Jacob (Dachshunds). Our Dachshunds were an especially distinctive pair, Lulu with her silver dapple color and Jacob with one blue eye and one brown.

That day, as they had every day for several years, the dogs ran ahead, smelling the morning smells and happily splashing through puddles, as it had rained heavily the night before. We walked the banks of the river and then headed slowly back toward the house. Picture this: Lulu's ears flying and coat gleaming, as she chased Jacob, mouth wide open and tongue hanging out, along a trail and through the trees. I will treasure that image forever because it was the last time I would ever see them.

Lulu and Jacob weren't with us when we got to the house, but this wasn't unusual. I was certain they would come running for breakfast any minute, but they didn't, and so we began to search. We made flyers and posted them all over our small town. When we checked with our neighbors, one had been out working in his yard all morning while his Pit Bulls played in a field, but he said he hadn't seen anything. Another mentioned he noticed a person put a canoe into the water at our landing that morning. Could the boater have taken the dogs?

I showed Lulu and Jacob's pictures everywhere, but still nothing. As days turned into weeks, my faith that we would find them became more and more difficult to maintain. I cried often, especially at night, because I missed Lulu and Jacob so much. When I picked up my purse to go out, there was no Lulu, racing for the door, excited for another car ride together. The cold, empty space where she used to curl her sweet warmth in the crook of my knee was a constant reminder she was missing. Our house was strangely lonely without them.

About a month after Lulu and Jacob disappeared, my neighbor called to tell me that the Pit Bulls down the street had killed her Cocker Spaniel. A while later they killed another small dog. Not only was I shocked and heartsick for the families and their pets, but my blood froze at the memory of those dogs playing with something in the field the morning Lulu and Jacob had disappeared. Could it have been my beloved Lulu and Jacob?

I still continued to search and hope, often looking on Petfinder.com in case Lulu and Jacob had been taken into rescue. Throughout my search I met many kind rescue people who encouraged me to get another Doxie. Not yet - I kept hoping for a miracle.

Just before Christmas, one of these rescue friends called and said, "There is a red, male Dachshund at the Salisaw pound. They don't have many cages there. When they are full like this, small dogs must sometimes be put in with large dogs. Sometimes this does not work out well..." She paused. "Could you consider fostering this dog until a home can be found?"

I felt the longing in my heart again for my Lulu and Jacob. What if this dog was Jacob? I knew it likely wasn't, but I heard myself agreeing to take him, just as a foster.

I immediately drove to a meeting place about an hour away. He wasn't my Jake, but the resemblance my new foster had to Jacob was remarkable, except that both eyes were brown. The dog's happy face and wagging tail warmed my heart. "Oh what a cutey," I thought, and was delighted when he snuggled right up to my leg in the car. "He's used to riding in the car."

Once home, my husband dubbed him JJ (Jake Junior). He got along great with Ruby and Shiloh, walked on a leash, and ran to the door when I got my purse. "Ahhh…" I thought, "…like Lulu." That night he wanted to come upstairs for bedtime so badly that I let him, and he jumped right in bed with tail wagging all the while.

At first, my husband was opposed to JJ in bed with us, but he relented because he knew how much I missed Lulu and Jacob. JJ snuggled right up with me, and it was such a wonderful comfort to feel his warm little body next to mine. That's when I thought I might like to keep him.

Shortly thereafter, my rescue friend called, excitedly telling me they had found JJ a home. My heart stood absolutely still and I wanted to scream, "NO, NO, NO!"

"But I was considering adopting him myself," I offered.

"Oh dear, I didn't know, and I have promised him to these people now. They have some paperwork to still finalize, but it looks good."

I quietly agreed to bring him back on Saturday, then hung up the phone and burst into tears. Of course, he ran right over and tried to comfort me, wagging and offering kisses.

I cried harder.

With JJ in my arms, I feel asleep that night feeling like I would like to just run away with him. It turns out I didn't have to because on Friday, my rescue friend called again to tell me they had encountered an issue with JJ's potential family. She asked, "Do you want me to put him back on the website, or will you adopt him yourself?"

Are you kidding? I just cried, "I want him, I want him," over and over again.

That was two years ago. JJ, now "Teddy," rides everywhere in the car with me and sometimes even accompanies me to work. He's a goodwill ambassador, greeting everyone he meets with a wagging tail and doggie smile, and he joyfully accepts the dogs we've subsequently taken in as fosters.

The answers to the mysteries surrounding the disappearance of my precious Lulu and Jacob elude me to this day. Did the Pit Bulls kill them? Wouldn't we have heard something if that was the case, though? What about Teddy – wasn't somebody missing him? He seemed so familiar in our home, but had no collar or microchip, and as far as we know, nobody has searched for him.

In any case, I am so grateful Teddy came into my life just when I needed him the most. We've since moved to a new house with a fenced-in backyard that keeps our animals safe. It opens to a five-acre field that we all enjoy *together*. I still keep an eye out for a blue-eyed, red male or a silver dapple female, but my other eye is always on Teddy.

 *Kathy Martine*

The Fainting Goat

Paige was on the table about to be euthanized. Picked up as a stray and almost bald, she had so many fleas that the shelter workers said her skin looked like it was crawling. They thought nobody would want her because she looked so bad, so there she was, on the table, minutes from the end of her life.

As luck would have it, just before the deed was done, the shelter director walked in and asked if Dachshund rescue had been called for Paige. That one phone call saved her life.

All Texas Dachshund Rescue put Paige into foster care with my friend Janice, who called me to rub it in because she knows I am a sucker for wirehair Dachshunds. My first introduction to Paige was through a car window. Her foster dad was dropping something off at my house, and she was along for the ride. Paige snarled and growled at me as I stuck my head in the car window. I thought, "Boy, she sure is mean and doesn't like me!"

A few days later, I was more formally introduced to Paige at Janice's house. She was a totally different dog, wanting attention, belly rubs, and to be held and cuddled. I fell in love and knew right then she was going to come live with me, even though I already had three other dogs. I couldn't take Paige until I closed on the house I was in the process of buying, but a week after we moved, Paige came home.

Honestly, Paige has not been the easiest dog in the world. She has many issues including a calcified disk in her back and arthritis in her knee, which gives her a funny little hop when she walks. She's had several teeth pulled, a bout of mild pancreatitis, and allergies to everything. She's always itchy - sometimes to the point of scratching holes in herself – even though I slather her with lotions, creams, and anti-itch medications. She is the most moisturized dog in the world!

Paige is wary of strangers and barks at them to stay away from her. However, once she is finished yelling at someone she rolls at their feet for a belly rub.

Paige's funny quirks, like her "fainting goat" impression, make up for the more challenging ones. If we hold our arms out for her to come to us, she immediately falls over and goes belly up like a fainting goat. She does it when we put her harness on, too – it's a scream! We put it over her head, and she falls over. We set her back up, put one leg through, and she falls over. We set her back up, put the other leg through, and guess what? You've got it, she's on the floor. It continues until you can finally get the whole harness on and buckled. Of course, she falls over again when you try to put the leash on. We laugh about it, but it's sad – Paige's odd behavior is probably due to abuse in her early years.

The most endearing thing about Paige is that her tongue does not fit in her mouth. When I sit her on my lap for a sincere conversation, she looks back at me seriously. But then the tongue slips out of her mouth and just hangs about a half inch down - I can't help but laugh! Yes, she's a goofball, but the important thing is that when she snuggles in to my arms, gives out that huge sigh, and goes to sleep, I know she feels loved and secure. It fills my heart.

Paige has come a long way from being that bald, unwanted dog that was a heartbeat away from death. She just needed someone who would take care of her, despite all her issues. For me, I love her all the more because of them, not in spite of them. I wouldn't change Paige for the world, which goes to show that there IS someone for everyone. Paige is just perfect to me!

 *Kim Stirrett*

A Long Pause...

Keep on Truckin': Kiwi was found running in a field. We adopted her during her heartworm treatment and were supposed to keep her quiet for a while. This was tough since any sign of a squirrel has her up a tree, swinging on vines like Tarzan, to get to the squirrel. She wags her tail furiously at any 18-wheel truck that goes by, so we have surmised that she must have been riding in a big rig, stopped at a rest stop, gone after a squirrel, and never looked back. -*Eleanor Williams*

HR Hound: We wanted a Dachshund companion to share in our adventures, so we adopted a very spunky, 13-year-old girl named Mabel who was up for anything. For three glorious years we camped, swam, traveled (she flew across country 12 separate times), walked the beach, and lived in a teepee and on a shrimp boat. In between journeys Mabel came to work with me and played a key role in our staffing decisions. If she didn't like someone when they walked through the door, they didn't get a job. Period. (It was the owner's rule, not mine!) -*Natasha Lane*

Petri and the Pilot

"Chicken killer." That's what they called him. It was the reason his owners gave when they dropped Petri off at a shelter in South Texas. They said he killed chickens, but then again, he was seven years old, no longer a fun puppy, and heartworm positive. Who wants to spend money on that? So off to the pound he went.

Diamond Dachshund Rescue of Texas (DDRT) was completely overwhelmed - foster homes and the kennel building were both full. But on the faith that there would be space for Petri once he finished heartworm treatments, a volunteer was sent to rescue him.

And space there was. Petri came to me and immediately brightened our lives. He loved his toys. I mean he really loved his toys. It didn't take me long to realize that toys were all this dog had in his life for a very long time. The other dogs really liked Petri and tried to get his attention, but Petri just played with his toys. It took a while for him to start hanging out with his siblings and seeking attention from my son and me.

Petri blossomed into a sweet, fun dog. He loved to play catch and would try his best to talk to me. I loved his growly voice. Now that he was happy and healthy, a new "forever home" needed to be found - Petri deserved it.

Along came Max, a retired fighter pilot. At 74 years old, he was told by his kids that he was finally old enough to have his own dog and not just dog-sit theirs. His daughter read Petri's description to him from the DDRT website and he felt an immediate kinship with the dog, as if his instincts were guiding him to meet Petri.

I love fostering rescue Dachshunds, but each one takes a piece of my heart with them when they are adopted. I want each one to go to the perfect-for-them home, and Max sounded perfect for Petri. I scheduled a time to get Max and Petri together, but first I had to say goodbye.

Petri's favorite toy was a squeaky tennis ball, but he had worn out the squeaker in his, so I decided a farewell shopping trip was in order. We stopped at the farm supply store on our way to meet Petri's potential new owner. Petri strutted into the store and was elated at the floor level bins full of toys! He climbed right in, searching for a favorite. Squeaky tennis ball found, he happily carried it to the cashier, bringing smiles to everyone who saw him. I picked him up so he could give the cashier the toy to ring up. She laughingly handed it back to him, and I announced that he was going to a new home. Everyone wished him well.

Back in the car, I looked at a happy dog playing with his new toy, and the tears streamed down my face. This joyful dog, destined to be put to sleep for killing chickens, was now bringing happiness to everyone... which was soon to include his new owner Max.

 *Cynthia D. Smith*

Braydi Joins the Bunch

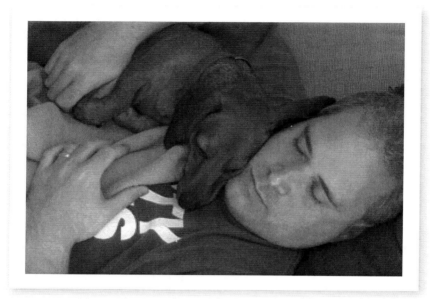

You know how some people comment about having their first child, and that child is so perfect they decide to have another - only to find that the second child is a little more, well, not-so-perfect? That was our experience with Braydi. Our first Dachshund, Bayley, was perfect: loving, good-natured, and well-behaved. Our second Dachshund, Braydi, was, well... much more of a challenge.

Braydi had been turned over to Coast to Coast Dachshund Rescue because her first "mom" found herself in a tough situation. Unexpectedly divorced, she had to work multiple jobs that kept her away from home for hours at a time. Braydi was kept crated and not socialized with other dogs or humans.

For some reason, Braydi was not afraid of Bayley, and they became instant friends. But when it came to humans, Braydi would bark so much she would foam at the mouth, and nothing could get her to settle down except barking herself to the point of exhaustion. A phenomenal dog trainer taught us how to socialize Braydi, and how to show her that humans are not all that scary. Having to live within our large family helped the socialization process, too, because Braydi was more than happy to accept treats and (ultimately) affection from everyone.

It has now been two years, and the difference in Braydi is amazing! The once-terrified dog who lacked socialization and confidence is now happy and carefree. She is still a little nervous around strangers until she gets to know them *or* until they offer her a treat. Our vet, neighbors, friends, and family are all amazed at how far she has come.

I have to admit that Braydi is my biggest accomplishment – she makes my heart want to burst with pride. Watching her romp with Bayley and our cats or play with our niece and nephew brings a tear to my eye. Braydi is proof that rescue works, and that love, patience, and persistence (and treats) can give terrified, unhappy dogs a new "leash" on life!

 *Robyne Gioco*

The 13 Days that Will Last Our Lifetime

We adopted Baron and his sister Abby from Hearts United for Animals when they were six years old. Baron had been an expensive dog – requiring back surgery for Intervertebral Disc Disease (IVDD) at the age of four – and so the pair was surrendered by their owner due to financial hardship. Baron also had a heart problem and contracted a virus the week before we went to get him. He was so sick that he refused to eat and lost four pounds (he was only a 13-pound dog to begin with).

We brought him home and hoped he would recover, but his heart could not take the strain the illness put on it. Two visits to the highly skilled vets at Texas A&M could not reverse or lessen its devastating effects and on the morning of his 13th day with us at 8:14 am, Baron crawled into my arms to give me the first kiss of our association and the last one of his life. He put his head down on my chest, his heart gave a stutter and a thump, and he was gone. He tried so hard to stay with us but passed of a massive heart attack.

Though it had been only 13 days, Baron had a lasting impact on our lives. We believe that Baron knew it was his time and stayed with us just long enough to give Stomper, our other disabled Dachshund, the courage to walk again, and to ensure his sister Abby was safe in a loving home.

Stomper swam very well using his back legs but refused to move them on land. By putting his nose under Stomper's rear end, Baron was able to lift Stomper up and push him around. To our surprise, Stomper started walking again, which he might not have done if not for Baron. He's wobbly, but we'll take it!

With that first and last kiss, Baron demonstrated that he knew he was home, loved, and in our hearts forever. Baron is buried in our front yard with a rose bush that is forever to be known as Baron's Rose. A beautiful, red rose bloomed a week after Baron's passing, and the bush continues to bloom throughout the winter, reminding us of the lasting impact Baron's few days with us had.

 *Southwind Kane*

The Entertainer

About a year after we lost one of our three Dachshunds I began to look for another. I searched for a reputable breeder, looked at shelters, and scoured the Internet. I finally came across Florida Dachshund Rescue's (FLDR) website and then waited for the right dog to show up. As I continued to monitor the website, we prepared for a new dog by allowing FLDR to complete a home visit and reference check. (In Florida adopting a Dachshund is more involved than adopting a child.) One day I saw a gorgeous three-month-old puppy named Heath and thought I had to get him. I knew my chances were slim and did not want to get my hopes up because puppies, like babies, are in high demand, so

I waited a few weeks to see if the words "adoption pending" would appear beside his name. When I finally inquired about Heath, I was astonished and excited to find out that he was available. Transportation was arranged to get him from New Orleans, LA, to my home in Milton, Florida. It took some time but after about a month-and-a-half, when he was five months old, he finally arrived.

It didn't take long to find out that Heath is quite the entertainer. First, he loves new clothes. Heath runs to the door and dances around whenever I come home with a bag in my hands. I dressed him up for a day at the park for our annual Barktoberfest in Pensacola, and he caught the eye of the activities coordinator for the Alzheimer's facility where my grandmother had been cared for. Now he entertains the residents there, too.

Heath knows when he is going to "work," and gets excited when we are about a mile away from the facility. Dressed up or "naked," the residents enjoy him so much that we visit once a week. Spaghetti Day is always his favorite because he gets to clean the spaghetti off any of the residents who might have some left on them. Occasionally someone will grab him by the neck or not want to let him go, but Heath has such a good temperament that he never snaps or growls.

Heath's role as entertainer doesn't end there. At home he sits up on his hind legs like a groundhog for his favorite toy, an empty paper towel or toilet paper roll. He frequently checks the roll in the bathroom to see if it's just about empty, and if he hears one being changed, up he'll sit, begging for the empty one. If I change it when he isn't in the house, I even save the empty roll, putting it on the garbage can lid for him.

As soon as he comes in, he grabs it and runs around showing off his grand prize, then plays with it for hours. He has such a fan club amongst our friends that they even save their empty rolls for him.

His groundhog imitation is not only reserved for empty rolls - he does it for everything. When we are sitting on the couch reading (or doing anything besides paying attention to him), Heath stares at us. If we don't acknowledge him, he puts his front paw on our hands. If we still don't acknowledge him, he sits up. He knows that will get our attention because he's so close to the edge of the couch he might hurt himself if he fell off. If we are getting ready to go somewhere, he follows us around, and if we stop for a second, he sits up in front of us. He sits up in front of the refrigerator, in front of the cabinet where the treats are, and even on the bed when he wants us to get up in the morning. It has become quite ridiculous, but is so irresistible - and he knows it.

It's hard to believe that somebody didn't want Heath and just dropped him off at a shelter shortly after he was born. We're lucky he didn't know how to sit up yet, because they never would have been able to let him go. Now that we have Heath, we cherish every moment and are thankful to FLDR for bringing us together. Heath's an "endless roll" of entertainment, joy, and love, and continues to enrich our lives and those of the Alzheimer's facility residents.

Christy Bateman

When Dachshunds Fly

A few weeks before Christmas I took in my first foster, a "blind," six-month-old puppy. The puppy mill he came from had the nerve to tell our rescue group to buy him for $50 or else they would end his life – such is the spirit of giving. Well, we weren't going to let him die, so a transport volunteer picked him up and met me an hour or so north of my house. The first thing I noticed was that it seemed like he could see, despite his deformed eyes.

As Christmas approached, we visited my in-laws, taking our family of five dogs (including fosters) with us. We stayed at the very pet-friendly La Quinta Inn, whose only pet fee was that I bring the dogs to the front desk to visit. While we were there, my in-laws came so close to adopting Hoover, which was my hope. But something stopped them - they saw that Hoover had picked me to be his forever mom. He was only my first foster, and I was already "failing fostering 101," as they say. He was never going to be re-homed – he was going to stay with me.

It was on that trip when Hoover confirmed he could see. We were in the hotel room when he caught sight of the dog in the mirror. Oh my heavens! He wanted to get to know that dog SOOO badly. His determination was like none I have ever seen.

We quickly found out that Hoover also has super-sonic hearing. His eye doctor loves to give him the peripheral vision test, where he drops a cotton ball to see if a dog can see to the side. Hoover doesn't see it, but the second it hits the ground, he looks at it. His amazing hearing is also demonstrated at home, where he goes from sleeping to *flying* out the doggie door in the blink of an eye. Whatever he charges and barks towards is always a mystery to the rest of us, including the dogs. It makes me laugh every time!

If someone had told me Hoover would be such a super-dog when I first heard about him, my response may have been, "Sure, when Dachshunds fly." Well they do – my Hoover is proof!

 *Zandra Clay*

A Long Pause...

Roomba®, Dog's Best Friend: Louie's game is to "hide" miniature, squeaky tennis balls around the house. He puts them on low shelves, books on the floor, places like that – retrieving them immediately so he can play some more. One morning, Louie put his ball on the start button of our Roomba® automatic vacuum cleaner. You can imagine his surprise when it sprang to life. This was the first time his "playmate" had ever moved! Dogs usually hate vacuums, but could the Roomba® become dog's best friend? *-Cindy Byers*

Almost a German Shepherd: I was warned that Peppe possessively protects whomever is holding him, but my excitement got the better of me, and, rather than approaching carefully as he lay in his foster mom's arms, I charged in. Predictably, Peppe bit me, very casually, with all of his five remaining teeth! Since we made a blood pact he had to come home with us, and he's spent his time guarding *me* ever since. *-Natasha Lane*

The Life of Riley

ere I was in my forties, and the only dog I'd had in my adult life was gone. I couldn't believe it. How could I think about replacing my beloved Dachshund-mix, Bailey? Would my heart ever heal? I missed the way he curled up next to me in bed, knew when I needed a kiss or a cuddle, and was fiercely protective yet gentle as a lamb. I missed him, and though I knew I could never replace him, I also knew that there was another Dachshund out there that needed rescue, another Dachshund that was meant for me to love.

As I am disabled and in a wheelchair, it's impossible for me to navigate the Oregon Dachshund Rescue building. Therefore, the dog chosen for me was brought to the car and passed through the window. He was a gorgeous, long-haired, red Dachshund but very much underweight with an air of neglect about him. Apparently, he'd been left outside *every* day and night for his entire two-and-a-half years. He was not socialized either. And yet, one look into those soulful, brown eyes, and I was in love again.

My husband and kids were also in the car, and after we had met our new pup, we began discussing names. His original name was Brownie, but he was redder than he was brown, and, honestly, the name didn't suit him at all. We were all throwing out names and calling him with each choice until I said "Riley." That was it! He immediately responded and has been answering to his new moniker ever since.

I was afraid my wheelchair might spook him, or worse yet, he'd get in the way of it and be hurt. I needn't have worried. From the very beginning Riley has acted as if he were trained as a service dog. He keeps me company, lets me know when someone is near the house, plays with anyone who shows interest, and even throws and chases his toys by himself for twenty minutes or more! Riley makes me laugh and cry with his love and antics, making the long days in bed, and in pain, seem more bearable. He loves burrowing under the blankets, and just feeling his warmth against me keeps me from being lonely.

The rest of the family sleeps upstairs, but Riley stays downstairs with me. Before we sleep, however, he does go from room to room, checking to see that everyone is safe in bed. Ever the lover, when my parents visited recently, he climbed up on the couch where my Mom was sleeping and pulled the covers away from her face to give her a good night kiss. When he was done, he came over to my bed and cuddled with me.

During my many hospital stays I hear that Riley stays near the front window watching for me. He refuses to eat and cries for me. When I finally arrive home, he runs outside and makes a beeline for my car door, then jumps inside while my husband gets my wheelchair out.

Is my sweet boy a replacement for Bailey? No. No dog could ever take the place of my angel pup. Just like children, each dog you love is different and irreplaceable. However, Riley has helped fill the void in my life that Bailey had left behind. He loves me unconditionally, listens to whatever I have to say, and seems to understand how I feel. He knows what I need before I do, and he is always there to keep me company. I can't imagine my life without my cherished friend.

 *Deb Cashmore*

The Most Expensive Movie Ever

I took my hubby Jamie out to lunch and a movie for his birthday. We had an hour to kill, so I went shopping at Target® and Jamie went to Petsmart® to look for a dog kennel for the back of our truck. He wanted it for when we take our Dachshunds, Scooby and Shadow, hunting.

Jamie rounded a corner and there they were – adoptable dogs from a horrific puppy mill that had recently been raided. There were Poodles, Shi Tzu's, and this ugly, scruffy, balding, sack-of-bones, black and tan Dachshund who no one was even remotely interested in – except Jamie. His name was Mike, and he had heartworm, kennel cough, and was very underweight. He sat scared and shivering in his crate, and wouldn't make eye contact with anyone. Regardless, Jamie now knew just what he wanted his birthday present to be.

Jamie left Petsmart® and immediately hunted me down to show me his birthday present. We returned to find an employee holding Mike. Was she adopting him? She sighed and replied, "Nope, I just wanted to get him out of the crate. No one wants him."

I turned around and my big, bad construction worker was crying! We stood there for close to an hour:

Me: *He's not going to be housebroken.*

Jamie: *I don't care.*

Me: *He's not going to be socialized.*

Jamie: *I don't care.*

Me: *He's going to cost us a fortune in vet bills.*

Jamie: *I don't care.*

And so, Jamie's gift to himself that day was a sad sack-of-bones named Mike.

Fast Forward One Year:

Enter one sleek, shiny, gorgeous, little, black and tan heart-stealer! Mike's heartworms are gone, he has lovely breath as the result of *two* dental cleanings, his hair has grown back in, and he is happy and content! On the downside, he tires easily as if he were a senior, even though he is only three years old. His little body had been through so much stress and there is only so much we can fix. We provide him everything he might need to be as comfortable as possible: dark places to hide, warm laps, and nine other furry brothers and sisters to play with.

Did we have to potty-train Mike? Yes. Was he unsocialized when we got him? Yes. Did he cost a fortune in medical bills? Sure. He ended up being way more expensive than that movie we were supposed to see, but with Mike, there are no credits rolling: the entertainment never ends.

 *Sandra Voyles*

Badgering Rats

When we adopted Reese, he fit right into our home, bonding with us and his new brother Bailey. However, Reese wasn't like our previous dogs.

You see, I've been active with dogs in obedience, agility, etc., but Reese was never into any of that. While researching the AKC website, I came across information about Earthdog, a competition open to Dachshunds and Terriers that requires them to exercise their hunting instincts. They travel down a tunnel to find quarry in a den (rats in a cage) and then bark and dig at it for the hunter (me). The more I read, the more I thought it was something that Reese would love. He was always nose-to-the-ground during our walks and very prey-driven.

I found a local "Introduction to Earthdog" class and signed us up. Wow, was Reese a natural. At the advice of his trainer, I got Reese a PAL (purebred alternative listing) number with the AKC, which allows unregistered dogs of registered breeds to compete in AKC performance and companion events, including Earthdog tests. Then we began entering trials.

During our first two trials Reese qualified and got his first title. Later that fall he got his second. That was last year. This year we are three trials in, and we are only one leg away from his Master title. This, according to our Earthdog club president, will be the first time in our club's history a PAL dog has gone so far. Sadly, Reese is not eligible for Field Trials because he is a rescue.

However, Reese and I love Earthdog trials because they are truly about having fun together. It's amazing to see Reese excelling at what his breed was meant to do. At home he's the sweetest, most cuddly, couch potato dog, but at trials he's strictly business. Just last month, he was clocked at three seconds to the rats (about 20 feet). He was the fastest dog in our class for that day. Now if only I could get him away from the rats so quickly - he'd be happy to sit and torment them all day!

 *Jill Diorio*

Fishing for Ranger

Since turning 40, birthdays seem to come more frequently and are harder than they were before. A particularly hard one to take was my 49th birthday, which I celebrated with several friends at our favorite Mexican food restaurant in Houston. We ate (and drank) Sunday brunch there and then headed home.

As I turned into the driveway, my neighbors ran up to me, yelling that one of my dogs had escaped and was underneath the house across the street. I panicked and forgot my rescuer motto, "Always take a head count," and hurried off to join the search.

For over an hour, we called, coaxed, and begged this black and tan Dachshund to come out from his hiding place and back to the safety of his foster home. It wasn't until someone suggested we try BBQ brisket that we actually made some progress. As I lay my stomach with the plate of food, the Doxie finally started edging closer. I felt like I was fishing for him, and the brisket was my bait. It worked, and after a few minutes of concentrated dining, the opportunity provided itself for me to slip a leash over his head. The dog was mine!

It wasn't until we were out from under the house, in the light of day, that I found out the dog was, in fact, not mine. I had never even seen him before! Nevertheless, I carried him home, gave him a bath, named him Ranger, introduced him to the others, and made him a promise that life would get better from that moment forward.

Several potential adopters came to meet Ranger over the next year, but Ranger blew it every time. He sulked, looked bored, and refused to participate with the prospective family. He was clearly not interested in going anywhere.

On my next birthday, the big 5-0, my friends surprised me with a party and another afternoon of margaritas and birthday wishes. My most treasured gift was the adoption contract for Ranger, the dog who met me, his mom, while lying on my stomach under a house over a plate of brisket after way too many birthday margaritas!

 *Linne' Girouard*

A Long Pause...

Wiener Takes All: After adopting my foster, Lucy, I found out she was a little quirky. She's become notorious for sneaking food off plates, eating an entire box of chocolates (yes, we called the vet), and bringing horrible "trophies" into the house (no more doggie doors). One night she wouldn't come when I called her for dinner, preferring to just sit on the couch. I thought she was sick until I noticed all six of the eggs I had just gathered from the chickens were gone. Lucy had hidden them all in the couch – they were to be her supper.
Eleanor Williams

Stubborn and Persistent? Not Me! I love Jack a little too much and am the culprit of his obesity. Recently I've cut back on what I feed him and eliminated treats, but it's hard when he looks at me with those big brown eyes and that sad face. What makes it worse is how insistent he is. Not only does he run through the house with his empty food dish in his mouth until he finds me, he then throws it at me! If I continue to ignore him, he beats the floor with it. What's a guy to do? I guess a little treat won't hurt... *-Willie Mosbrucker*

My Lucky Charm

L ucky was indeed fortunate the day my friend found him on Craigslist. Boys from his own family had beaten him on the back with baseball bats, causing four disc ruptures and spinal injuries that resulted in Lucky losing control of his bladder, bowels, and back legs. When the owner finally took Lucky to a vet the next day, the vet recommended x-rays, pain pills, and medicine. Upon learning that the vet couldn't "fix" him, the owner refused all care, took Lucky home, and relegated him to the yard. She then posted the following on Craigslist: *Six-year-old, male, neutered,*

silver dapple Dachshund, $250.00. Paralyzed, to be adopted immediately or will be put to sleep on Monday.

My friend saw the Craigslist ad and called some rescues to see if they could take Lucky in, but no one could. Their foster homes were already overflowing and Lucky needed immediate attention. In desperation, my friend called me to ask if I would take Lucky if she could get the owner to surrender him. I agreed, and my friend succeeded in rescuing him from his heartless family.

Our homes were four hours apart, so we met in the middle to transfer Lucky into our care. He was listless, unresponsive, and in severe pain, which put me in tears. I had doubts about his survival but am not inclined to give up easily. Something told me Lucky would live if I could convince him he was safe and loved.

When we returned home, we bathed Lucky to get rid of the fleas, feces, and urine that had attached itself to his fur. His dull, lifeless eyes were full of pain, so we gave him some pain medicine. He would not eat or drink, so I placed the food in his mouth and massaged his neck to get him to swallow. I then got water down his throat with a children's medicine dropper.

Our vet was also concerned for his life because Lucky was dehydrated, dangerously underweight, in severe pain, and unable to have surgery because it was too risky for a dog in his condition. Regardless, I still believed in Lucky. Maybe he would not walk again or regain control of his bladder and bowels, but he would live - I refused to accept anything else. The vet gave us pain meds and antibiotics and wished us the best of luck.

For three months we forced Lucky to eat and drink. Then, one morning, when I sat down on the floor with him in my lap, his tail wagged. It wasn't much, but it moved! Things have been different ever since. A month later Lucky started to eat and drink on his own – he just stuck his nose in the food one day and ate it. At the same time he began to regain control of his bladder and bowels. That was when I knew Lucky decided to live again.

Lucky began to gain weight and is now at an appropriate 27 pounds. I tried to exercise his back legs so that he could use them again, but it appears Lucky is not so fortunate in that department. Instead, Wayne from Disabled Dachshund Society of Georgia built Lucky a cart. This has given Lucky access to the whole house and yard, including the birds and squirrels he runs across the grass to catch. Lucky is now a gentle and loving boy who adores being brushed and petted. He's no longer in pain, his eyes are bright and shiny, and his expression is filled with love.

Lucky may someday walk again, but even if he doesn't, he can still live a full, happy life with his cart. He has not been able to overcome his fear of children, but he has become a role model for surmounting adversity. When Lucky came to us, I was experiencing my own challenges due to a lifetime battle with Lupus, the loss of my child, and complications from two previous heart attacks and a stroke. I was hurting, tired, and ready to give up, but caring for Lucky wouldn't let me. He showed me that I have a reason to live and that my pain and hurting is just a test of courage and determination. I'll be forever grateful to my friend who brought us together. Lucky is the charm that gave me back my will to live.

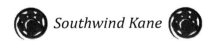 *Southwind Kane*

Sound the Alarm

Gunther's owners died within sixteen days of each other leaving a six-year-old dog alone in the world. No one in the family wanted him, so he went to a shelter in Austin, Texas where he was about to be euthanized. Luckily, he was rescued and placed in foster care in North Texas. The only catch was that he was a shy dog and the home already had over a dozen other dogs living in it.

The foster called us to ask if we could help him downsize by taking in Gunther. As experienced fosters, we understood Gunther's predicament and knew we had to help – such a crowded environment would not afford Gunther the attention he needed and could impede his chances for adoption. I agreed to take Gunther in, and my husband and

I drove through the snow to get him. My husband wasn't thrilled that we had gone to so much trouble for a dog with "no personality," but I saw something special in Gunther. I just didn't know what it was yet.

Both of our previous black and tan males had been named Cato, so we renamed our new dog C.J. for "Cato Junior." We quickly discovered that C.J. is a loner. At first he didn't like to be picked up or loved on, but after a time has allowed us to pet him. He's a little awkward indoors because his last home had kept him as an outdoor pet, so he prefers to sit in a comfortable bed on our front porch for several hours a day. Little did we know that his penchant for our porch would lead to him saving our neighbor's life.

One Sunday night at 9:00pm, C.J. was sitting in his usual place on the porch when he sounded an alarm with his bark. I quickly went outside to find my neighbor, who lives several acres away, yelling in pain. Her two female German Shepherds were fighting, and in her effort to separate them, they had turned on her. By the time we arrived, she had puncture wounds in her arms that were bleeding profusely, and the nerve in her finger, which had gotten caught in her dog's mouth, had been crushed.

We put one Shepherd in the house, left the other in the yard, and controlled our neighbor's bleeding as best as we could. I then drove her to the closest hospital, which was about 15 minutes away (an ambulance would have taken too long). She was hyperventilating and I knew she could go into shock at any time, so I drove the bumpy, winding road as fast as I could while trying to keep her calm and conscious with soft words. It was a close call; she passed out just as I pulled into the emergency room. When she came to, she called her husband who ran home to administer first aid to the dogs and then met us at the hospital. She recovered completely, and C.J., of course, has become her favorite dog.

I feel like C.J. came to us to accomplish this special mission, for our neighbor and for himself. They both know he was instrumental in saving her life, an act that has since given C.J. confidence and purpose. Since C.J.'s heroism, my husband and I have a newfound respect for him. We see wisdom in his eyes that we overlooked before.

 *Glenda Watson*

Near and Far

I am filled with excitement. Today, my daughter and her husband arrive for a month-long visit!

Sadly, they lost their home and most of their belongings to the Witch Creek fire in southern California. Then, while still trying to recover from that blow, my daughter's husband Richard was laid off from his job. Trying to make the most of things, they decided to turn these seemingly devastating events into a wonderful adventure by using their insurance and severance money for a dream trip around the world. But before they leave for this fabulous adventure, they'll stay a month with us: Mom, Dad, and a whole lot of dogs!

I foster rescue dogs, primarily Dachshunds. Megan and Rich also love dogs and dream of the day when they will have their own. Rich has never had a dog, and Megan lost her beloved Dachshund, Winnie, several years back. She passed in the prime of her life from a brain tumor – a very hard loss for Megan.

For the next time around, Megan knows just what kind of dog she wants - a longhaired, dapple, female Doxie. She's always loved wee-wee dogs (her nickname for the Dachshund breed). Needless to say, the kids were happy to spend their time with us playing with Tika and Bones, our foster dogs, and our own pack: Teddy, Ruby, and Shiloh.

We are a week into the visit and having so much fun, when I come home from a trip to the market to find Megan, looking a bit worried, but also excited. She says, "Mom, Ginny called, they have an emergency." (Ginny is my rescue friend.)

"Oh?" I asked, "We're pretty full."

"Yes, but Mom, it's a dapple Doxie girl..." Her eyes tell me she wants to jump in the car right then. "I told her, we would take her," she offers hesitantly. I guess we're off to pick up another dog!

On the way to the shelter, Megan fills me in on what she knows. Apparently, this is one terrified pup. The owners who surrendered her said she is sick and needs to be put down, but our contact at the shelter doesn't think so. Upon our arrival, the contact meets us right away and says, "She's not able to take this environment. She won't eat or drink. Actually, I can't even set her down."

Meg takes one look at the dog's huge eyes and terrified expression and then gathers up the mess of black and white, mottled fur into her arms. Once home, Meg is able to make the scared little dog eat and drink a bit, but the dog can't keep the food down. After successfully feeding her some baby food, I suggest Meg crate her for the night, but Megan has other plans. She holds the dog tight and heads up to her room.

In the morning I hear Meg get up early to take the new one out. Thus begins a love affair. Megan names her Bailey, and they spend much of their time together. My daughter, who has lost so much, all her physical memories burned - her wedding dress, her photos, the quilt her Grandma gave her, all the little things, gone - now has a new purpose in life. In just a few days, Bailey is scampering about the house, walking on a leash, eating and drinking, and running and playing. There is no doubt, Bailey adores Megan.

All too quickly our month together ends and we wonder how Bailey will react to Megan's departure. Megan worries too and finally says, "Mom, I have a huge favor to ask. Will you keep Bailey for me? I want her to be my dog forever, but the trip is planned, and we can't change it now."

And so they go. Bailey sleeps on Meg's bed for a week. She waits at the door every day but slowly comes to me more and more. Soon she is sleeping with us, and I love her sweet spirit curling gently against my back at night. Bailey helps me feel close to my daughter even though she is a world away.

Weeks turn into months, and Bailey grows happier and healthier. She comes to love the whole family. My older sons have to work at it a bit, but soon Bailey warms up to them, too. I hope Megan will decide to make her home near me instead of returning to California because I know I will miss Bailey. (Oh, right, and I enjoy time with my daughter, too!)

In the meantime, we find wonderful forever homes for Bonz and Tika, and we foster and re-home four other dogs. In a flash, Megan and Rich's year-long journey comes to a close and they are on their way back home to us for another wonderful month-long visit. We can't wait to hear all about the trip and see photos. We feel so blessed our daughter is back in the USA, safe and sound! But will Bailey even remember her?

They arrive in the afternoon. Bailey is out in the backyard playing with a chew toy and her new friend Layla, one of our latest fosters. Bailey hardly looks up as Meg comes out on the deck and calls her name. However, a second after sniffing Meg's feet and then her hand, Bailey turns over on her back and wiggles around. She remembers, no doubt.

By evening I am chopped liver - the old momma. Megan and Bailey are joined at the hip! Megan marvels at how happy and healthy Bailey has become. Although my daughter was traveling a half a world away, Bailey is the one who has gone far. She is now miles away from the scared, little barnacle we peeled off our friend at the shelter. Gone is the hollow look in her eyes. Instead they are filled with a sparkle and a zest for life. She has become a beautiful, vibrant, healthy canine companion.

Megan did take Bailey back to California, and so I miss them both. Bailey is happily enjoying the beach, hiking, and long walks in her new neighborhood. She even has an Australian Shepherd "brother" named Kirby to keep her company now. Although we are again all far apart, I hold the memories of the time we spent together very near and look forward to the next adventure.

 *Kathy Martine*

Jewels in the Desert

J ewels' story before coming into rescue is very sad. Unfortunately, it's also very common. Like many Dachshunds, she went down (the common term for a dog with Intervertebral Disk Disease - IVDD) and needed back surgery, which was paid for by the original owners. When Jewels did not regain control of her bowels and bladder, the owners decided to chain her in the backyard, smack in the middle of the Texas summer. Jewels had nothing but stagnant rainwater to drink and scraps to eat. For shelter she had to crawl under the porch.

Fortunately, Dachshund Rescue of North America (DRNA) rescued Jewels. They flew her from Dallas, TX to a foster home in Fredericksburg, VA, that specializes in caring for "down" Dachshunds. Yolanda, the foster mom and IVDD "expert," had Jewels treated at university veterinary hospitals for parasites and injuries to her legs from crawling around outside. Jewels received the best care possible.

A few months later Jewels made another flight, this time from Washington, DC to Las Vegas, NV, where we were eagerly awaiting her. She came to us weighing only eight pounds but was free of all parasites and loves to eat. Jewels vacuums her food down like no other dog I have ever seen, not even bothering to chew.

Jewels immediately charmed us all and became the apple of her daddy's eye. She put on some weight - maybe too much - which soon forced me to put her on a diet. A skillful, holistic vet, using acupuncture, magnetic therapy, spinal adjustments, and special supplements, had her walking and running in no time (albeit like a drunken sailor)! Now she loves her walks, and every morning makes sure I know that she's not to be forgotten. She never cries or whines but often gives us a "rrooorrooooowwwww" and a bark – that's how we know she is happy.

Needless to say, we love Jewels with a passion. Whoever named this little girl may not have known it, but they hit the bull's-eye - she really is a jewel. To them she may not have been a diamond in the rough, but to us she is our Jewels in the desert!

Thank you, Yolanda, for saving her and for trusting us with her. I'm indebted to you forever.

 *Vitoria T. Ferraro*

Hold on To Hope and You'll Find Gracie

My husband Ron was working odd hours which completely threw off our daily routine. He had to be to work by two o'clock, so we went out to our Tennessee pastures to check on the goats and sheep earlier than usual. Gracie Girl, our ten-year-old Dachshund, KD, our eight-year-old yellow Lab, and Taz, our six-year-old Blue Heeler, all ran out to the yard with us.

Gracie immediately went under the chicken coop where we had baby ducks (she loves baby-anything and will sit under the coop for hours just watching them). We left the three dogs at the gate while Ron and I went through a small pasture to our barn to check on three nesting turkey hens because the dogs made them nervous. At the barn we visited our goats and sheep, which are protected by our Great Pyrenees, Milly, who lives with them. Seeing that everyone was happy and healthy, we gave Milly a belly rub and headed back out to the yard. Strangely, we only had two faces peering through the fence at us when we returned. Gracie Girl was nowhere to be found.

My heart started to race because Grace was always waiting for us. Ron and I searched our pastures for three hours until Ron had to leave for work. Our youngest daughter, Kara, took over the search in the afternoon, but we still couldn't find Gracie. The neighbors hadn't seen her, either.

I spent that whole night watching for Gracie to come home. Her disappearance made no sense to any of us – in ten years she had never wandered away. What possibly could have happened?

I reported her disappearance to our local sheriff, vet, radio station, and shelter the following morning. Then I spent the day making posters and had Kara hang them at stores and at churches. For a week Ron and our neighbors searched the woods while I hung back at the perimeter calling Gracie's name. We went up and down nearby roads and gave her picture and our phone number to everyone we saw.

Days turned into months and there still was no Gracie. I kept an eye on the Petfinder website in case she was found by a rescue, but she never appeared. I had just about given up hope until one day my husband suggested I check the website one more time. Though it seemed futile, I logged on, and to my surprise, shock, and disbelief, there she was, in full color! All American Dachshund Rescue (AADR) had posted her under the name of Shannon, but it was definitely my Gracie Girl. Because I couldn't find a phone number to call, I sent pictures and descriptions to anyone associated with the rescue to tell them that she was my dog. When Kara and Ron returned home to see Gracie's picture on Petfinder, Kara started crying and Ron wanted to know where she was. Can you believe that the answer was Michigan?

It wasn't until nine o'clock that night that Ruth, the women who was fostering Gracie, called. Pointed questions about Gracie ensued, and Ruth confirmed that the pictures we sent looked just like the dog she was fostering. Believing us, she agreed to e-mail Diane, the president of AADR, to see what they should do. After thanking her, I woke Kara and Ron up to tell them the great news.

The next morning was my real test, as Diane was skeptical, and she put me through the ringer. It took our local shelter and our vet to convince her that "Shannon" was actually Gracie, but after careful investigation she not only agreed, but also arranged transportation for Gracie to come home.

In discussing how Gracie ended up in Michigan, we discovered she'd shown up on a porch where she hung around for a few days. The property owner took Gracie to a vet in Dover, about thirty miles from our house. Why Gracie left our yard and how she made it that distance will forever remain a mystery. The vet referred the property owner to a local rescuer when he scanned Gracie for a microchip and turned up nothing. The rescuer subsequently contacted AADR, which is when Gracie's journey from Tennessee to her foster home in Michigan began. During her two-month adventure Gracie took a long road trip to Michigan and back, met many caring volunteers, and got a vet check, dental cleaning, and microchip. It's amazing that she could be gone for so long and then returned to us in as good, if not better, condition than she was in when she got lost! Truth be told, though, had she been microchipped in the first place most of the heartbreak and drama would have been avoided.

When I got off the phone with Diane, I cried like I've never cried before. KD, Taz, and my daughter's dog, Roscoe all came to console me. I was overjoyed to tell them that Gracie was coming home!

The day of Gracie's return couldn't come fast enough. It was Diane who would meet us with Gracie in a PetSmart® parking lot (her husband had been in Michigan visiting family and brought Gracie back with him when he returned to Tennessee). We arrived at the drop-off point in time to watch them arrive. When Gracie saw us and felt Ron's touch, she immediately recognized us. She licked Ron's whole face and then did the same to me.

After we dispensed with the formalities, Gracie jumped up on her seat in our truck like she had been there just yesterday, and her tail wagged all the way home. She became even more excited as we pulled into our yard, so we let her out to potty before the rest of her family came to greet her. There was so much tail-wagging and licking!

Gracie seemed to settle back in, but it didn't take long for her to disappear again. This time, however, when we went looking for her we found her in the bedroom, curled up on her bed, sound asleep. Gracie was home, and we were never going to lose her again.

 *Marsha Manos*

Beep Beep.....

I was driving home from the store one afternoon when a weird idea just popped into my head: "My next dog will be named Wylie Koyote!" I had three dogs already and no intention of adding to my pack, but there it was – a new name for a new dog.

A week later, Barbara from All Texas Dachshund Rescue called me and asked if I could foster a little wirehaired puppy for them. He had been dumped during the most horrendous of thunderstorms and came in to rescue as a stray. Anybody who knows Barbara knows she can be a bit of a devil when asking someone to foster, often placing dogs with fosters she know will "fail" to rehome them and will instead provide them with a wonderful home for the duration. She knows my soft spot is wirehair Dachshunds, which is why, in this case, she called me.

I usually prefer to take in older or special needs dogs because I know that puppies can always find homes. Oh, and puppies are difficult! When I picked up my new *foster* puppy, I realized that he fit the "special needs" category. He was pitiful looking with big, sad, brown eyes and a tiny, blond mohawk on his red head.

At home, I told my husband, "Don't get attached. He is only here temporarily. He will find a home quickly." But still we gave him a name – Wylie.

We'd only had him for two days when out of the blue, Wylie became very lethargic, and by the next day he was vomiting. I rushed him to the vet, and x-rays revealed that he not only had pneumonia but probably distemper, too. Wylie was a very sick little boy. The vet asked how far we wanted to go with him, and thankfully Barbara said to do everything possible. The rescue group was not going to give up on him.

Since it was late and my regular vet was closing, I had to take Wylie over to the emergency vet for the night. There he received some intense treatments, including antibiotics, IV's, nebulizers, and chest palpations to loosen up the gunk in his lungs. Thus went the next few weeks - from the emergency vet in the mornings, to the regular vet during the day, and back to the emergency vet again each night. (You can imagine what this was costing the rescue!) X-rays continued to show scar tissue building from the distemper, but Wylie looked and acted like a normal dog. Lucky Wylie - even if the x-rays weren't showing it, his treatments were working.

Finally, Wylie was allowed to come home. I quarantined him from my other dogs, just in case. They had been vaccinated, but I didn't want to take a chance. My husband felt so bad for little Wylie that he slept with him on an air mattress downstairs in his quarantine so Wylie wouldn't be alone.

Just like the Road Runner kept reappearing to the cartoon Wile E. Coyote, my Wylie's illnesses proved to be more difficult to get rid of than we thought. He had a slight relapse at the same time my husband and I had plans to leave town. We decided the best place for Wylie was at the vet while we were gone because they could properly care for him. Wylie's treatments continued and his health improved. Four days after we returned, he came home. He showed no signs of neurological problems that normally go with distemper, and after 30 more days of strict quarantine, he was declared fit. Finally he could come out and meet the rest of our "kids." The only lasting reminder of his sickness is that he now has no enamel on his teeth, so they stain very badly.

Wylie had finally beaten his Road Runner, but what did that mean for us? His picture was now on the adoption website, but could we just let him go after all we had been through? My husband complained that because *he* was the one who kept Wylie company during his quarantine, *he* should get to keep Wylie company now that he is well. The decision became easy - Wylie was already home.

During his treatment, Wylie cost the rescue several thousand dollars, which Barbara makes him pay back... In kisses! That's right - now that Wylie is a very healthy two-year-old, he serves as one of the kissers in ATDR's kissing booth fundraisers. He's quite proud of his job and does it very well!

 *Kim Stirrett*

Kaiser Roll

So adorable with those big, soft, floppy ears and such soulful eyes, but SO fat! Who could have overfed and under-exercised this little guy? Dachshunds love to eat, but their backs just aren't designed to support such a barrel.

We decided to rescue this little Dachshund from a life of obesity. We named him Kaiser Wilhelm Maximus, aka Wilhelm the Great. This name seemed more appropriate than Pork Roast, as was suggested by my son. For short, we called him Maximus.

Kaiser seemed happy enough but initially resembled a lump. We persuaded him to part with about 20% of his body weight, despite his foraging in the yard and "hunting" apples and plums that fall from the trees. I even found Kaiser with a green tomato from my garden one time! (I spoke seriously to him about that.) Since he's lost weight, his personality and agility have shone through.

He is sweet, well-behaved, loyal, and loving. He is three years old, but given his former girth, we suspect he had never been for a walk. On his first excursion, he wound down to a very slow pace after about ½ mile. Now, six months later, he can do a five-mile hike and is always raring to go.

He supplements his hiking with other activities such as dragging blankets and pads from his and his siblings' crates, and either bringing them to the living room or hauling them outside through the doggie door.

He also has a penchant for what we call "dogerwauling." As a siren sounds on a nearby street, he points his nose to heaven and howls like a wolf. With no disrespect to his regal namesake, we can't help but laugh out loud!

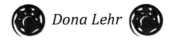 *Dona Lehr*

(Does your Doxie need to lose weight too? See how Kaiser did it in the next section: "The Doxie Diet.")

The Doxie Diet

Obesity is a concern for many Dachshunds – they're little, and they love to eat! And, let's face it, they're not exactly known as long distance runners. From the guardian's perspective, resisting adorable pleas for treats can sometimes be next to impossible. But, as we all know, when the health of our loved ones is at ~~steak~~ stake, we need to feed them the right diet. Here's how one of our contributors, Dona Lehr, helped her dog Kaiser Wilhelm Maximus to become a little bit more, well, Minimus.

Morning:
- 1/4 cup high quality dog food
- 1T plain yogurt

Evening:
- 1/4 cup high quality food with a couple of doggie treats on top

Snacks:
- A Cheerio or two
- A little bit of cheese now and then.
- No other intentional human food (don't feel bad if occasional accidents happen - sometimes things get dropped...)

The key to helping an obese dog lose weight is good nutrition, exercise, and persistence! Check with a vet to see if this diet might be right for your dog.

Wieners Awry

IVDD, You Can't Stop Me! I thoroughly researched Intervertebral Disk Disease (IVDD) after adopting a paralyzed dog named Skippy. I learned that "down" dogs struggle with their weight and so I looked for ways to give Skippy more exercise. I couldn't afford pet therapy, so putting him in the tub to swim was the next best thing. Surprisingly, in a few inches of water he "walked" with all four legs - it was as if he had no paralysis! Over time the swimming has helped to build muscle and keep down Skippy's weight, eventually leading to him taking a few steps on his own outside of the tub! Though he tires very quickly, he now stumbles around on carpet or grass. Swimming in the tub was an inexpensive therapy with amazing results. *-Angela Johnston*

As Loud as a Rose Is Beautiful: Rosie was found in the woods after she most likely escaped from a puppy mill. Because of her past, she was not well-socialized, and it took her quite a while to respond to her name and get potty-trained. Additionally, Rosie barked *loudly* and *incessantly* when I put her out to potty in the yard. Patience and love has worked miracles. We never punished for poops in the house. Instead we made sure she got out a lot, and carried her right outside with a firm "NO" when we caught her in the act. As for the barking, I started putting Rosie on a leash to go out in the backyard so that I was right there with her. If she barked, I put my hand over her snout and said, "NO." If she continued, I picked her up and brought her inside. I can't claim she's

Wieners Awry

100% quiet now, but even off-leash she immediately stops when I say, "NO." No complaints from the neighbors, hurray! -*Anonymous*

Seeing Decisions Clearly: Spirit was already blind from detached retinas (probably hereditary), but one day I noticed his right eye getting cloudy. It looked like a cataract, which is no big deal for a blind dog, but my gut told me to take him to a specialist for a check-up. I'm so glad I did, because while it *was* just a cataract, a pressure test revealed 48% pressure in his left eye (it's supposed to be around 10%). More investigation found he also had glaucoma in the left eye and was possibly developing it in his right. We discussed treatment options but really they were just delay tactics. Because of the pain the pressure was causing, and the likelihood it would also affect his other eye, Spirit's eyes would have to be removed. We discussed prosthetics, but they are more for the humans. My blind dog would probably prefer to live without them since we would have had to put drops in his "eyes" every day, so we skipped them. In the end, the only thing Spirit lost, so far as he's concerned, was pain. –*Zandra Clay*

The Light Will Shine Through: When we got six-months-old Lucas, he had been living in a crate his whole life. He didn't know how to play, was afraid of our touch, and would dash off at the slightest movement or sound. Since this was our first time helping such a timid, insecure dog, we looked to a local therapist for advice. She taught us how to use the T-Touch method, which is similar in some ways to massage, to help calm Lucas' nerves. She also set up a beginner agility course in our yard where we helped Lucas build confidence and learn to have fun. Liberal use of treats has been instrumental in the positive changes we've experienced in Lucas, but they are also the result of patience and tenacity (on our part and that of our dogs). Four years later Luke is still watchful and afraid of sudden movements and sounds, but he is otherwise playful, loving, funny, and courageous. The name Lucas means "bringer of light," which is truly what he has been. Each gain he makes brings us joy and touches our hearts. *–Trish Rivera*

Tag Number 19

J erry and I are owned by many puppy mill Dachshunds we have fostered and adopted through Colorado Dachshund Rescue and other rescue groups. They moved in when the grown kids moved out, and now they are our "kids."

This miniature Dachshund, Mariah, spent six years breeding in a Tulsa puppy mill until her rescue. Her head had been permanently marked with a branding iron, her little ears had notches in them from metal livestock tags, and her legs were forever crippled from living on wire in the mills for so many years.

Mariah never knew that she wasn't a Dachshund show dog. She had no idea her head was any different because of the brand. Her notched ears were perfectly normal, as far as she was concerned; and she took pain pills only when her legs were so bad that she couldn't do the "Dachshund strut." To herself and to us, she was the perfect Dachshund.

Sadly, Mariah left this earthly world at the "young" age of 21 in May 2007. For 15 years, Mariah was our shining star and the queen of our house. Along with her paw prints on our hearts, she left a legacy:

Mariah Hope would like to dedicate this poem to her puppy mill-rescued brothers and sisters, and to all the abandoned, unloved, and forgotten dogs that will spend their lives in the horror of a puppy mill.
Bless you, little ones. All of you.

My name was always just "Tag Number 19."
The saddest puppy that you'd ever seen.

I lived in a place that was terribly sad.
I felt like my owner was always so bad.

There were so many dogs that lived in my cage.
Old ones, young ones, dogs of every age.

My house was made of wire, you see.
There wasn't much room for others and me.

So many cages were stacked up too high.
We couldn't see out. We always would try.

Summers were hot, winters so cold.
So hard on the young ones and also the old.

I didn't have sun. I didn't have heat.
So many times, I had nothing to eat.

Sometimes I'd get water from a dirty old jug.
My cage and my skin filled with all kinds of bugs.

I was doomed to a life with nothing to gain.
But I kept on dreaming, again and again.

I wanted a family that loved only me!
I wanted to feel grass and see sky and a tree.

Is there a place for someone like me?
Or will I always be just "Tag Number 19?"

I must wear my tag all night and all day.
My name is "19" I'm not happy to say.

It tells my owner lots of things about me.
That's when they know I'm a mommy to be.

I have my puppies about two times a year.
They're always so cute and so very dear.

After a while they come and take them away.
There's never time to love, run, or play.

I wonder what happens to the babies I've had.
I hope they're not living a life that's this bad.

My owner was talking of a pet store one day.
"If you want to make money, this is the way:

You breed the dogs till they're sick or they're old.
Who cares if they're loved, if they're warm or they're cold?

As long as the money keeps rolling on in,
it's not my fault if they're hungry or thin.

These dogs are a business. Not meant to be pets.
Don't waste your profits on good food and vets."

Such was the life of "Tag Number 19."
She was the saddest dog that you've ever seen.

Then came the day of more puppies for me.
Something went wrong. They weren't meant to be.

All of them died. I'll never know why.
They took them from me. I did nothing but cry.

"She's too old to breed. Seems her time has come.
She's no good to me. Something needs to be done."

I'm only six. I have more years to live!
My life isn't over. I have so much to give!

Would this be the end of "Tag Number 19"?
Is she never to know about all of her dreams?

One sunny day, some folks came with a van.
"We've come from the Rescue," said the kindly young man.

All of a sudden they opened my door.
I'd never seen so many people before!

"Please don't hurt me" I wanted to say.
But they all smiled and said, "It's your lucky day!"

Soft, gentle hands took me out of my pen.
They hugged me and kissed me again and again.

My owner was handcuffed and taken away.
"It's Animal Cruelty!" I heard the man say.

All of us saw the sun, grass and sky.
Tag Number 19 had a tear in her eye.

I've never been held, I never got to play.
I'm getting a bath. What a wonderful day!

Now, I live in a house with a yard green with grass.
I watch out the window and see things go so fast.

I have my own toys and a very soft bed.
My new family loves me. I get pats on my head.

There are balls to chase and treats to eat.
Walks to go on and people to meet.

I don't know what happened to "Tag Number 19,"
Today my real name is Mariah Abby Marie!

 *Beth Casselman*

About Happy Tails Books™

Happy Tails Books™ was created to help support animal rescue efforts by showcasing the love, happiness, and joy adopted dogs have to offer. With the help of animal rescue groups, stories are submitted by people who have adopted dogs and then used in breed-specific compilations that entertain and educate readers. Happy Tails Books™ donates a significant portion of proceeds back to dog rescue groups.

Happy Tails Books™

To submit a story or learn about other books Happy Tails Books™ publishes, please visit our website at http://happytailsbooks.com.

We're Writing Books
about ALL of Your Favorite Dogs!

Schnauzer Chihuahua Golden Retriever PUG

DACHSHUND German Shepherd Collie Boxer

Labrador Retriever Husky Beagle ALL AMERICAN

Border Collie Pit Bull Terrier Shih Tzu Miniature Pinscher

Chow Chow Australian Shepherd Rottweiler Greyhound

Boston Terrier Jack Russell Poodle Cocker Spaniel

GREAT DANE Doberman Pinscher Yorkie SHEEPDOG

ST. BERNARD Pointer Blue Heeler

Find Them at Happytailsbooks.com!

Make your dog famous!

Do you have a great story about your adopted dog? We are looking for stories, poems, and even your dog's favorite recipes to include on our website and in upcoming books! Please visit us for story guidelines and submission instructions. **http://happytailsbooks.com/submit.htm**